FLIGHT

Cover Photograph © Lloyd Grotjan. Used with permission.
Edited by Marcie McGuire and Yolanda Ciolli
Layout and design by Yolanda Ciolli

Library of Congress Control Number: 2020901088

ISBN: 978-1-942168-33-1

Published by
Compass Flower Press
Columbia Missouri

Illustration credits:

Julie Scrivner, Watercolor, page 3

Bill Penning, Photograph, page 33

Ray Spenser, Photography, page 49

Ron Ehlert, Engraving on 1874 C. Sharps 45/90 replica, page 51

Hippos, Carved stone, artist unknown, page 87

Christening gown, c. 1902, page 107

Mzeona Iagorashvili, *Golden Grapes*, Wool painting, page 109

FLIGHT

COLLECTED POEMS

GREG P. BUSACKER

Compass Flower Press
Columbia Missouri

For Carol and Julie.

Dedicated to

Kit and Cathy Salter

Generous coaches with a stand for excellence
who enabled me to believe I could.

Table of Contents

Penned Imagery

The Living World

Worldly Pursuits

In the Best of Company

Tender Affections

Musings

PENNED IMAGERY

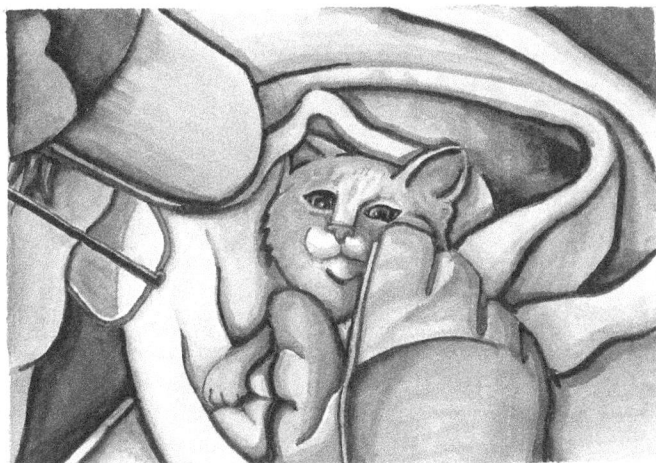

PENNED IMAGERY

Happy

I heard I was happy.
I realized it was true. And,
I was so happy being happy,
I almost cried.

August 7, 2019

Why Language Moves Me

I know why language moves me,
for without language,
thoughts and depictions
of love and beauty
would only show for some to see
and few to know.

It gives life to hidden passions
but without the uttered words,
thoughts be dead as in the tomb
where none give breath
to thoughts of old.

In bright light the words will dance.
Still, language spoken may not
convey the hidden magic,
for he who speaks
takes a chance
that those hearing
will not engage and
let the message go cold.

But should the words
connect the souls,
those who hear will
through the magic
of language know
emotions flowing in scintillating light
be it day or night.

Emotions of joy, pain, of love and passion,
when freed upon the public green
are as expressive as waves on a beach
softly breaking or with thunderous display.
Only language captures the moment for another day.

June 26, 2017

GREG P. BUSACKER

A Life of Love and Focus

Mother taught kindergarten for many years;
she was the oldest of eight children. Being familiar with
young children, she often found herself the arbiter
of equality. Any treat was to be divided equally and
bananas became a special focus, haunting her
into her eighties. She often asked the question,
"How do you divide a banana equally?"

Look at a banana's graceful shape
with both linear and curved sides with the volume
varying from end to end. It offers
a difficult challenge for equal division.

Since most people like to see equal serving portions,
the banana is given the evil eye by all who prepare
them for eating.

While it is too late for Mother, every fruit stand
in America should have a posted warning.

Warning!
Cutting this Fruit
Into Equal Portions
Will Drive You
Bananas!

August 26, 2018

Early Artistic Expression: Looking Back

Do you remember as a child
when you wanted to create
something beautiful to present
to a favorite person?

It always seemed that the
something never lived up to
the image created in the mind
before the presentation.

Yet the favorite always saw the beauty
you intended. As an adult, my writing is like that,
presenting the opportunity to silently acknowledge
my love and admiration for my favorites.
For written gifts create a space supporting
mutual exchanges, honors, and intimate interactions.

August 7, 2018

The Falconer's Landscape

With thanks to C. Stephen Heying

Our falconer is a surveyor
by profession, with a reach
beyond metes and bounds and local mapping.
His fascination with hawks and their training
enables him to experience life as the bird sees it
and to become part of the three-dimensional landscape.
When in the field with the hawk,
he is not only defining edges of parcels,
but immersing himself in the natural world
by participating in the taking of game at a primal level.

Those who hunt often dispatch a messenger
of death to interact with their prey.
The guidance of the messenger is a special skill set
learned by the falconer and the hunter.
The falconer sends a live hawk to take his prey,
while a hunter often uses a gun.
The training of the hawk
is the falconer's special skill-set
creating a unique partnership with the hawk,
such that the success or failure
of the hunt is shared.

The bird hunter on flushing a pheasant or quail
is responsible for bringing
the shotgun to bear,
so as to pluck the fleeing bird
from the air
with a cloud of directed pellets.
Similarities end there.

The bird hunter prepares his quarry for a meal,
cleans his shotgun and resumes his normal duties.
The falconer shares his take with his hawk
to cement their bond. Then he cares
for his hawk in his daily routines,
so that they may hunt again.

The relationship between hawk
and handler is built on trust.
From the hawk's perspective, there
is only trust or lack thereof.
The human relationship to the hawk is more complicated
as hope, awe, love, and pride are involved.
Hope for the possibilities of the hunt,
awe of the hawk's capabilities.
Love for the demands of required care,
training, and flying the hawk; and pride
for being a spokesman for the sport,
and the ability to train and teach others
what is needed for their success.

The practice of falconry requires
heavy emotional involvement.
The bird does not reciprocate love,
and many mishaps can lead to separation
or even death of the hawk.
Every falconer faces this possible loss,
which can best be described
as devastation for the falconer.
Recovery, if possible, is starting over with a new bird.

The rewards of the sport
are evidenced by its having been
an ongoing practice for thousands of years.
The falconer is immersed in the natural world
where animals are potential prey.
The acquired hawk comes from a class
of avian predators that live on flesh.
The falconer takes what the hawk does naturally
when it is flying free and trains it so that
it will take another animal
as prey and return to the falconer.
It is likely these acts will be repeated
as long as hawks and men trust one another.

March 7, 2019

The Westward Explorer

Many the night around the fire
he had listened
to his elders speak
of remote lands,
the visions they had seen,
the beauty of exotic landforms,
varieties of vegetation, and
the wonders of traveling alone.

When he came of age,
he joined the crew of a Viking longboat
destined for southern Greenland
and the colony of Eric the Red.
The journey was difficult and
he spent much of the time bailing.

On reaching the new villages,
he soon heard of an effort
to sail west and south
to reach a vast unexplored land.

Entering the mouth of a large river,
they continued to sail to the west.
Reaching an area of immense rapids and falls,
they grounded the boat
on the southern shore.

On shore at last,
he walked while thinking
of the seas they had crossed
and the boat crew's prayers for deliverance.

He explored the coastal area
and found himself alone.
Slipping through the trees,
he followed a path leading west. Later,
when he returned to the longboat's location,
it was gone. He waited a couple of days and
when it did not return,
he decided to continue to the west on foot.

He found himself
in a land of endless forests,
many rivers and mountainous terrain.
After many days,
he walked into an open grassy park
covered by a vast vault of blue sky.
It reminded him of the ocean,
but he was stunned
by the seemingly infinite space.

Feeling insignificant and
exposed to unknown dangers,
he felt terror to be close at hand.
Then he remembered
how danger, undefined, fills the mind.
Putting down panic,
he noticed the wind moving grassy stands.
The movement was pleasing to the eye and
he could see the traces of the wind
crossing the plains.

Visually, the landscape seemed static
but looking closely, he found the subtle colors and textures
offering varied looks, for which he had no names.
In the far distances, mighty bison herds
stretched the horizons. Clouds of birds flew off the marshes.

One day, storm clouds gathered.
He took shelter in a shallow cave and
woke to the songs of birds. Lying there, he mused
on the circumstances that brought him so far.
Taking stock, he found his exploring days were over
as his strength was fading with the coming winter.

Surrounding himself with leaves of grass
he noted he had traveled far and wide,
taking directions from the stars.
His path left virtually no trace,
and all of him that would remain
was his knife and scattered bones.

He had found a land faintly touched by man.
And in time, others will come,
entranced by luminous lights flashing
in darkened seas, and prairies laced with wildflowers.
It is hard to foresee an end,
but eventually, even time will bend.

January 16, 2019

Learning to Fly

As a child you lay on your back in the grass,
watching the birds and the occasional airplane fly by,
and dreamed of flying. Later you learn fulfilling a dream
often involves standing in line.

In the Army when it seems natural to wear your
heart on a parachute, you find you are standing in line
in a roaring airplane. It seems you are part of a living,
bucking organism. Finally, the jump light turns green and
the line races for the door.

You launch yourself into the void, to fall free into silence,
to drift in dimensionless space toward an undefined earth,
landing with a controlled roll into another opportunity to
    stand in line.
But now you know the passion of flight while being suspended
by wings of cloth and string. For flying takes many forms,
    as do dreams.

December 17, 2016

Musings on Images

A poet was thinking about writing
and pondered the verbal creation of images.
He was reminded of a Christmas song—
and the words, "Do you see what I see?"
He realized, *the heart of poetic art,*
is to convey the image of thought
in words for the realization of another.
This creates a bridge between the
writer and his readers.
When the readers cross the bridge,
they enter another land.

March 26, 2017

A Fight for the Right

Once upon a time there was a Princess
who loved books and had little interest
in governance. Her father despaired
of her indifference, but took some encouragement
from her love of martial arts.

With her father's death, his aura vanished,
leaving the Princess to ponder what needed
to be done. Her enemies saw an opportunity to
take control of the kingdom and
massed troops to overthrow the monarchy.

The Princess quickly gathered and inspired
her own troops. She offered the enemy troops
a chance to join her. Disdaining their refusal
to accede to her demands, she proceeded
to destroy, humble, and humiliate them.

So the Warrior Princess vanquished her foes, and
sent the pretenders slithering to the edges of the battlefield.
She then announced, "There is nothing left to do,
I am retiring to my keep to incubate my books."
This pronouncement left her allies in confusion and disorder.

But not all were confused. The chief wizard happily
looked forward to the return of chaos and indecision. And
began to formulate his return to power while the Princess
wrapped herself in her books.

Both the Princess and the Wizard are on an unknown road,
each standing for their right to be. The question is,
when will they see the possibility of a partnership
in governing the kingdom. For each alone has much to atone.

July 3, 2019

The Elfin Glade

One morning at dawn,
while deep in the woods,
I felt an elfin power.

It took time and patience
but I enticed the elf
from his hiding place
using Haiku as bait.

The sighting surprised
a fun-loving elf,
who loves his people
and is always a step behind,
unseen except for flashes
of brilliance.

But the elf was angry
at being revealed. And
I had to pay two twenty-dollar
gold pieces to mollify him.
Plus, I had to promise never
to tell anyone what I had seen.

In turn the elf would continue
to maintain his peaceful glade.
And visitors would continue
to leave fulfilled.

Except for me;
I was no longer welcome.

February 22, 2017

The Sorceress's Vision

With Thanks to Geetha Davis, MD

Last night in camp,
the King was told:
"Your vision is cloudy, my Lord,
and it is affecting your hunting.
But I see there is a way to correct
your affliction. We need only to detour
past the Sorceress's keep and tarry there
awhile as she practices her art.

"She works with common things in
uncommon ways. I do not know
the mechanisms she uses.
But I have spoken with men
who do know, and their reports
are miraculous."

The King wondered about the cost
and value of this treatment,
but soon found himself at her keep.

On meeting him, she said,
"Your eyes are cloudy, my Lord."

The King replied, "Aye my lady, that is so.
But what can you do
and at what cost?"

The Sorceress continued,
"Being half blind is bearable
but you wonder at my fare
for treating you to see clearly.
My charges require your faith
in my work and in what I can
provide. Additionally, after your
treatment, I would be appointed
as an advisor to you."

"Initially, this will be a bold
move and it will cause you
to see the world differently.
But your rule will be
more just and the value
of my adaptive involvement
will set your court apart."

So based on trust, the King
found himself strapped
in a chair, head back, with
potions in his open eyes,
followed by manipulations
he did not understand.

The King's vision cleared as promised.
He incorporated the Sorceress's
council in matters of State,
and his kingdom prospered.

April 11, 2019

A Memorable Vacation

Uncle Bob was a large man.
What he lacked in height,
he made up in weight.
His body shape was rotund,
with the maximum
circumference occurring
at the belt line.
From there
it was tapered
up and down.

The big problem with such a shape
is keeping your pants up.
Uncle Bob did not like suspenders.
And he had discovered trousers with
a rubberized waist band.
He was then able to roll his shirt in the waist band.
The shirt was a kind of suspenders.
It worked well, too, with
a few minor failures.

My aunt and uncle decided to
take a winter vacation and fly
to Florida. Once on board,
Uncle Bob settled himself into an aisle seat.
This was a bad choice.

The plane reached altitude and
the fasten seat belt light went out.
Aunt May asked Uncle Bob
to get her sweater from the bag
in the overhead bin.

With considerable grumbling,
Uncle Bob stood, opened the bin door,

pulled out her bag,
and retrieved the sweater.

He had to lift both
hands overhead to put the bag back.
As he stretched to replace it,
his waist band unrolled. His
trousers dropped to the floor,
exposing the "whitey tighties."

His instinct was to grab the pants
but then the bag would fall.
So he had to endure gasping passengers
across the aisle as he reached high
to shut the bin.
Naturally, he mooned everyone aft
as he retrieved his pants.

For many, it was the highlight
of a memorable trip. Uncle Bob
never flew again.

May 1, 2017

What Was Hidden is Not Lost

When I was young and
searching for information,
I wondered why it was not available.

Now it comes to me unbidden,
stirring old memories of my searches,
and I am nearly unable
to do anything with this realization.

I could examine my newfound information
from the basis of what might have been,
using the possible outcomes
to seed the clouds of my dreams.
Then, as I drift towards sleep,
I could craft new adventures
to fuel my soul for the days to come.

For now, I see
what was hidden is not always lost.

September 9, 2017

Visiting the Sick

One visits the sick
and the world is compressed.
The now consumes you.

Visiting the sick,
a sense of duty and love
is hard to balance.

Duty is calling
and resentment can be close;
Love can be set aside.

Come with love expressed,
be there to appreciate,
and duty falls away.

Your visit is set.
Today your time is your gift;
know you will be back.

July 15, 2017

The Search for Common Ground

The search for common ground
rides the waves
of human thought.

As you slide from wave's peak to trough,
seeking company and
dreaming of actual conversation,

a third perspective
arises to become
an island for the speakers.

Becoming still in the island's lee
with a new understanding,
the sea no longer seems endless,

and the common ground
grows firm through
communication with others.

March 12, 2017

An Eagle Scout Creates Self-Evaluation

It started when he realized he did not know what to do
with his life: Do I work, go to Community College, do both,
or something else? Then he reflected on the training
given to him while earning his Eagle Scout Badge.

He asked himself: What do I bring to the table?
What organizational and planning skills
acquired in Scouts are needed to complete a major project?
If I am honorable and trustworthy too,
I must represent a very small minority of adults.

Those are all pluses he thought, but what if I
brought those skills to a new project called:
"What do I want to do with my life?"

He realized this was not something that
needed to be completed in a hurry.
But to avoid the swirl he had been in required
identifying different possibilities, and seeing
if there were projects or a mini project worth exploring.

All these explorations will suit the training
I already have. I have been told that I have the
skills most people would gain doing a Master's
or Ph.D. degree. Then after completing seven
to nine years of college, they find they are at
the bottom of a new heap. But now they know
how to think and so do I.
So it all rests on my own efforts.

I will conceive projects designed to explore the question:
"What do I want to do with my life?" And for each project, I will
examine the skills I bring to the table to evaluate whether or not
I want to spend any more time on this.

It is time to remember who I am.

September 23, 2017

A Meditation on Choosing Life's Path

"Your vision will become clear only when you can look into your own heart. Who looks outside, dreams; who looks inside, awakes." – Carl Jung.

I

When he was a young man trying to identify his life's line of work, he looked outward, relying on dreams and imagination, observations of family, friends, and adult members of his community who were doing things that looked interesting and valuable.

He had the tools available to everyone for changing life's circumstances. He could act on ideas, dreams, imagination, and vision for changing his own circumstances. But, while these sources offer an invitation for change, they are like shadows without the support of determination, passion, and purpose. These critical supports had yet to be identified for him. Further, he could not distinguish the difference between a job and purpose. If you had a job, then you had a purpose, no job, no purpose.

When he was looking at career work as an expression of fulfillment, two questions were often asked: what kind of job are you looking for; and what would you have to do to get where you want to be? He could not answer the questions, and he seemed to lack the skills to press forward on his own. So, he went to guidance counselors for insights on possible careers and the means of determining a suitable career and identifying what he wanted to do, as well as finding a purpose to realize his potential.

He did not achieve clarity this way, and while waiting for something to happen, he took a drastic approach. He dropped out of the university and caused a total change in his life by joining the U.S. Army. There he was trained as a helicopter mechanic and a paratrooper.

He enjoyed the work, but declined to make military service his career.

II

As he looked back on his life, two careers were attractive to him as a boy: an airplane pilot, or a professional baseball player. Both were dashed by a requirement for excellent vision. He also loved physical labor and would work with anyone who needed help. But that did not seem like much of a career choice. He was good with his hands and tools, but the answer to the question, "What do you want to do with your life?" remained in a fog. He wondered if he needed therapy or specialized courses promising outcomes of knowing who you are, etc. He was suspicious that they would not deliver the promised outcomes.

After military service, he took a job as engineering assistant on a soil survey crew. He was quickly able to see how vital it was to finish his degree. Back in school, he studied in areas where he had been told he had an aptitude. He completed a Bachelor's degree, a Master's degree, and a Ph.D. in Biological Sciences. He was now trained as a Biologist for field and laboratory investigations and research. Had he found a career?

He was forty-three years old when he realized he was in a career he liked. He was working for a state transportation agency as a Natural Resource Specialist. Several years into the job, he realized that his statements of what he wanted to do had come true. He had once stated that he wanted to act as a liaison between the transportation design engineers and the regulatory natural resource people in state and federal agencies. Even so, he had been largely unaware of his shift in awareness that made the role possible; he had developed the capacity to understand both areas. He was truthful; and he was persistent in finding what was possible to build in time and budget.

III

He then took classes that trained him to look within his life to distinguish who he was and who he wanted to be. The focus of this training was inward, where before, the focus had been outward. He now knew his concept of purpose had been evolving and he could authentically say: "My job is not me, it may be an expression of me, but my purpose will go on after the job ends. For instance, my purpose is to be in touch with people and be aware of their wants and needs."

He discovered changes from inward self-examination may come slowly or quickly. He found there is no clear path to self-discovery. Knowing change will happen no matter what, his journey to discovering his purpose went more quickly when he continued to work on expanding his purpose beyond a job description. Finally, he awakened to who he was in the world with people and circumstances. Now he was able to contribute wherever he was. He no longer had to worry that he may wake-up wondering what happened — to his job and his purpose.

IV

He was now in the fourth quarter of his life. He retired from his transportation job and moved to another state to run a small farm. As he aged, the range of activities he could accomplish on the farm diminished. But, one area of expansion was writing. He started writing poetry and within eight years it became a major force of his self-expression. He published one book and was working on the second with nearly eighty percent of the material needed already written two years after publishing the first book. He wrote about what inspired him and subjects he had wondered about. The range of subjects was broad; people liked the work he wrote. He found the exchange fulfilling. His poetry helped define his purpose by creating windows both into and out of his life.

His comfort with who he was gave him the freedom to accept his critics. It was a place he never imagined he could work from, and it was a place he would not have discovered without knowing who he was.

January 6, 2019

Fire: For Those Who Survived

Written for my cousins in Paradise, California, after forest fires destroyed the City.

In my imagination,
you are in a living hell
while the rest of humanity
looks on, or not,

while you strive to live,
having given up
your instincts
to save goods and property.

Experiences of life
in and during
a near-ultimate disaster
sear the soul,
but bring the opportunity
to experience life
as an adult,
without a list of grievances
or nonessential concerns.
Leaving you
thankful to God,
for the gift of life
in all its joys and sorrows.
And now you know without question
who you are
in the service of God and man.

I cannot imagine
the depths of your sorrow
from your losses
and the heights of the joy
you find in the survivors.
I do send you my prayers
of love and strength
for you in your life to come.

With all my love, Greg

December 6, 2018

Dim Bulbs Rule

Do I hate my light and love Congress? or
Do I love my light and hate Congress?

My light used to be dependable
but I never expected Congress to be so.

Was it envy that caused Congress
to banish the dependable incandescent light bulbs,
replacing them with the dim LED bulbs?

The push for equality has triumphed.

Congress will not be outshined.

Dim bulbs rule!

January 2014

A Ship of State

A new Captain assumed command
of the USS Executive Branch on January 20th.
He came to the office as a novice in politics.
Compared to professional politicians
his language was direct, and he was often
unaware of the difficulties he could generate
for himself and others by speaking his mind.

In part, his plain speech got him elected.
People were tired of political speech,
for professional politicians were steeped in evasive
language. Their rhetoric was nuanced,
full of omissions and half-truths, and they rarely
followed through on promises not to their advantage.

Previous holders of his office had spent
years in developing skin capable
of shedding all imaginable attacks; they knew
when to respond. Because he had not developed
a tolerance for verbal attacks, he was prone
to retaliate in similar abusive language, which
had unintended consequences. In one sense he was
correct, his attackers were out to destroy him, though
many thought his Twitter account was his worst enemy.

He was surprised to realize his enemies would
go to any extreme short of murder to incapacitate,
emasculate, and/or render him powerless.
From the perspective of his enemies, the good
of the country seemed not to matter unless it matched
their vision. In the war of words, the possibility of
partnership in governance became a fleeting fantasy.

Getting underway, the ship navigated treacherous shoals, occasionally becoming stuck while waiting for the tide to turn. Meanwhile the bureaucrats continued to follow existing policies, and it was as if nothing had changed; AI (Artificial Intelligence) had come of age.

February 22, 2107

THE LIVING WORLD

The Rain

When rain falls on a man
in its many forms,
it is sometimes welcomed,
often cursed, and mostly
endured. But some seem unaffected
by the falling rain.

How can this be? Are there individuals
who are able to walk between the rain drops?
The question conjures the image
of a man moving with such fluidity
that he is not wetted by the rain.

But maybe passing through rain
is not a question of wet or dry;
rather it's a question of an attitude
being displayed by those moving
through, who are unaffected by the wet.
While they are aware of the rain,
they are unconcerned, because
the rain is the rain; that is all.

January 26, 2019

Cathy's Garden

Lying in a wooded glade,
Cathy's garden accepts all souls.
Some are transitory,
and some remain; but stay or go,
it's all the same. A shrine here,
a totem there, all laid out
with exquisite care.

The varieties of vegetation
suggest a sublime art form
of layered chaos coalescing into
a vision created from strata,
colors, hues, and textures.

Approaching the space
you find quiet and green.
The edges defined by solomon's seal
and lily of the valley. A resplendent
many-colored vegetated base
is formed from numerous varieties of hostas.

Deep in the garden, plants cast a blue-green
shade pool; flowers poke through,
blooming for the seasons.
Blossoms droop to gravity's call, others
stand true and tall. Many are obscure,
many bright, all beckon
from morning till night.

Standing in splendor, you find
it begins to work on you. And
you become aware of your
presence being accepted. Slowly,
you are part of it,
no longer a visitor.

GREG P. BUSACKER

You move along the pathway,
you change to fit the scenery.
At the end, you are
mentally and physically altered,
you leave in peace and with gratitude
for the world Cathy shares.

July 15, 2017

Frogs: Why We Study Natural History

Tom: We all know what frogs do, right?

    Jerry: Well, if we know what frogs do, how do we
    know it?

Tom: Because there is lots of information on frogs.
People have been writing and filming about
what they do and where for decades,
and we have documentaries on film and TV.

    Jerry: Let me get this straight.
    We know what frogs do because
    there is a vast amount of knowledge
    in a readable and visual format
    that anybody can look at
    and know what frogs do
    or should be doing?

Tom: Yep, it is all said and done.

    Jerry: Well, do you really know:
    What frogs are doing now?
    Are their populations stable?
    Does it matter if they are not?

Tom: Good point, but my only contact with frogs
is their spring calling which goes on for some weeks.
And occasionally I see a frog near water
or even hopping across the road.
How would I know if their populations are not stable?
Who monitors frogs and how are they funded?

    Jerry: Funding for monitoring probably
    comes from the natural resource agency.
    And I bet they really don't know much
    about existing frog populations.

Tom: Maybe they need to modify their genetically driven behaviors for easy monitoring. For instance, stop hiding every time someone walks by. Or they could sing all summer long rather than just in the spring of the year. In short, frogs could make it easy to monitor their populations.

Jerry: I thought you didn't like GMOs (genetically modified organisms).

January 6, 2017

Realization of a Childhood Dream

As a boy he read stories of the people in Vermont
working in the deep snows of early spring.
Using horse-drawn sleighs, they tapped sugar maples,
collected sap in buckets and made syrup from the sap.
So when he thought of maple syrup,
it was exotic, it was expensive
and it was wonderful.

He knew Missouri woods were not
teeming with large maple trees.
But stories and images stuck
in his mind. And in his seventh decade
he came late to the game, determined
to try the process anyway.
In the fall of the first year
he went to the woods
looking for candidate maple trees
to tap in the coming spring.

Tapping a tree begins the daily dance
of checking for collected sap,
the drip rate determines the daily volume.
As the flow responds to temperature's highs and lows,
one watches for days of sun-driven warmth
in Winter's blankets of cold, but too cold,
or too warm, there is no flow.

The gathered sap is subjected
to a preliminary forced evaporation.
As sap is heated to reduce water volume
and concentrate the sugar,
dense steam rolling off the wood stove
weaves in the air like manes of flowing hair.

This concentrated sap is filtered,
then further reduced with heat
to increase the sugar concentration.
As the brix is teased slowly upward

by the departing vapor,
the mixture deepens to a rich brown.
Finally, the hydrometer seems to levitate at the
magic line indicating the desired brix.

The finished syrup is bottled in hot packs,
stored in the refrigerator
and distributed to family and friends.

Having done so, he reflected.
It is never too late to fulfill a childhood dream.

February 17, 2018

Unintended Consequences

Early morning and I heard him coming.
There is something very distinguishing
about a centipede's walk: cascading
waves of little feet.

"What's up?" I asked.

"It's your wife, Sir."

"What about her?"

> "Well, as you know, I am the fifth in the line
> of Centipede Kings since your arrival
> ten years ago. The deal was, we would manage
> the floor critters for number and variety and you
> would leave us alone."

"Yes, I remember."

> "The problem is your wife is ruthlessly
> killing floor critters. Before she
> got her new eyes, she couldn't see them,
> and now she does. We can stand a few losses,
> but we are running out of high-grade food.

> "To make matters worse,
> the Floor Critter Union has filed
> a complaint alleging excessive pressure.
> The balance is upset, and for some bizarre reason,
> the floor critters have taken to the daylight
> and hiding at night.

> "To deal with this, we are bringing in
> outside help, and we are going to cull the herd
> to clean it up. But please, ask your wife to BACK OFF!"

"I can do that, but please speed the cleanup.
She is an impatient woman."

"We will do our best."

A short buzz of many feet and he was gone.
True to the Centipede King's word,
the mercenaries went into action, and
there were so many dead,
even I could see them.
We vacuumed for the next two days.
My wife took off her
stomping boots
and rested.

With the crisis over, my thoughts
turned to catching a newly arrived mouse.

June 6, 2017

Merlin the Parrot, Sings His Adventure

With a Nod to co-authors Serena Howard, and Carol Busacker

I escaped the parrot cage,
landed in a tree
wondering what happened to me?

Down below I hear my Mistress sing,
           "No hawks, no owls,
              why won't you come back to me?"

I shouldn't have been so bold
regretful I am
the night was frigid and cold.

Freedom seems to have a price,
I dream of peanuts
and miss my food and water.

Do I become a cannibal?
Walk on the wild side?
And eat my avian kin?

Or, go back to ease and greed,
peanuts and fruit?
Lordy, Lordy clip my wings!

April 4, 2016

The Deer Hunt

Inspired by Jose Ortega y Gasset's Meditations on Hunting

I   Preparation

The life and death struggle
between predator and prey
will be joined this day by the hunter,
who is the top predator
on his farm.

His passion to be a participant
in the natural world[1] drives him
from his bed three hours before dawn.
Today's hunt for the White Tailed Deer
will fulfill his desire
whether or not he kills a deer.

He chose his location
to wait for deer, drawing
on his knowledge of
their habits and habitats.
Checking the weather before
leaving, he believed his
observation site overlooked
areas frequented by deer.
Moving to his stand
in the dark, he settled in.

II   The Hunt

As increasing daylight
filtered the view,
it seemed as though he was
watching empty space.
The first half hour nothing moved.
By sunrise, the bird activity was chaotic.
The local Red Shouldered Hawk

stopped in a nearby tree. Birds were
flying everywhere and some
nearly landed on the hunter.

Pileated Woodpeckers seemed to be
laughing at his determination
to shoot a deer. As time neared
eight o'clock he was beginning to
agree with them. His confidence
in seeing a deer was ebbing.

After sitting for an hour and a half,
his discipline to stay put until
the chosen time paid off. At
three minutes to eight
a deer appeared in the berry
patch. She was standing still
and looking around. Briefly she
looked at him then looked away.
He brought the rifle to his shoulder
firing one shot. She collapsed in a heap
and the taking of the game was over.

III   Processing the Prey

He began to focus on the next phase,
processing the prey for consumption. He
ensured the deer was dead.
Then he headed for the house for
a cup of coffee and a planning session
on how he would proceed.

First, he headed for the four-wheeled
mule which he had recently serviced.
Starting the engine, there
was a massive oil leak at the filter.
So he shut it off and headed for
the tractor. The battery was weak
and it would not start. So he
drove the pick-up, and field
dressed the deer.

Remembering his father's lesson,
and noting a large horizontal limb
on a nearby oak tree, he tied a
rope to the deer, then passed it over
the limb, and positioned the deer
so that when the truck backed up,
the rope would pull the deer into the truck bed.

In doing so, there was a loud crack and bang.
The limb broke off the tree and fell
onto the truck, putting a new dent in the cab.
Simultaneously disgusted and amused, he tied
the deer to the bumper and pulled it down
to the building, and hoisted it off the
floor for skinning and butchering.

IV   Consumption of the Prey

He believed that processing
the animal was part of the hunt.
He recalled his father's dictum as
appropriate: "Eat what you kill."
It took effort to skin and cut up
the meat, and it made him appreciate
what he was doing. Finally,
the last quarter was cut up, packaged,
and frozen.

Consuming the prey was the last
part of the hunt. And in the coming
months as they ate the deer, he would
appreciate the animal's gift to his
family. He had been hunting for
seventy years and his passion to
spend time in the natural world
had never abated.

December 12, 2016

[1] Jose Ortega y Gasset, Meditations on Hunting, 1972
Charles Scribner's Sons; First English Edition

A Bufflehead Duck Takes Flight

With a jump and a run,
a Bufflehead Duck
takes flight.

Lifting wingbeats
and running red feet,
crossing the water
making skipping-stone splashes
and images sweet.

Now out of water
with wing tips so close
mirrored images show
not a drip or a splash
from above or below.

We watch in wonder as
this little duck
takes to the air
on a day so fair,
and we thank the gods
we were there.

December 31, 2016

With Permission
© Ray Spenser

Hannibal: A Confluence of River and Time

Our annual get-together was set
for mid-June in Hannibal, on the
the Mississippi River, known for its
mystic and historic power in America.

Now waters flow our way,
warmed during the long-twisted run
from the northern bogs of Minnesota
and fields of snow,
arriving here at Summer's eve, and
to us they show an opportunity.

We board the local riverboat,
with imaginations filled
with Samuel Clemons, Huckleberry Finn,
the call of 'Mark Twain,'
and surrender to the river.

Our journey is carried forward,
and though it be momentary,
we float on these waters
as they travel to the south,
basking in their given gifts
for a short hour or so.
But to us, it seems as though
we are riding the flow of time.

Drowsing with sun-driven dreams,
sweat running in our shirts,
buoyed by the mighty water's surface,
We know we are alive
in the heart of our nation.

June 18, 2017

WORLDLY PURSUITS

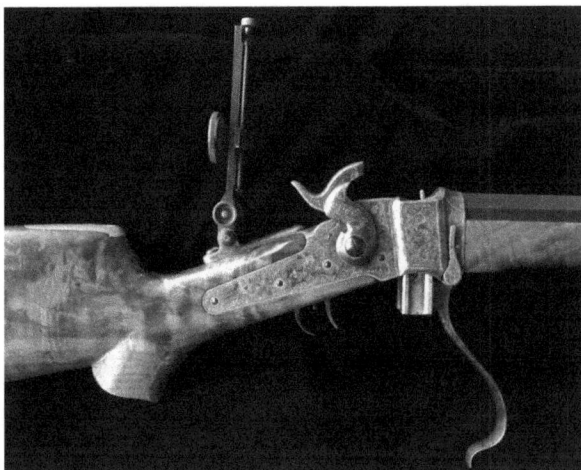

1874 C. Sharps 45/90 replica

Learning to Write

When he was four, his parents called him the little man.
He wanted to write, but they would not give him a pen.
So he took his big boy pencil and made representations
of geometric shapes while grinding the graphite into the paper.
"That's nice," he was told. He knew it was not.

The next Christmas, a small box contained
a dipping pen point, pen point holder, and a bottle of ink.
"Wow," he said, "now my writing can be like Mother's."
Then his parents said, "It doesn't come from there, it comes
from you. The pen is a tool to capture your thoughts,
and it is up to you to express them beautifully.
The pen will do the job if it is handled correctly."
This caused him to forget the pen was a gift.

He had noticed that his mother's pen did not run out of ink
in the middle of words. She said, "This is a fountain pen.
When your penmanship improves, we will get you one."
He practiced with his inkwell bottle, dipping the point
while guarding against excessive ink, drips, and blobs.
When his birthday arrived, he received a fountain pen.

All the lessons learned were put to use.
He studied the secret to filling the new pen's ink sac.
True to expectations,
he could write more before running out of ink.
But the pen leaking in his shirt pocket
was an added worry. He complained to his father who said,
"Be careful what you ask for." He found the advice confusing.

Then next wave of improvements came from ball-point pens.
They seemed a better option, but the points accumulated
a ball of ink and paper fibers which might be deposited
at the end of a sentence, on your shirt, on your fingers,
or on some other place where it was not wanted.

Then came the fountain pen with disposable ink cartridges.
He suffered the expensive low-volume cartridges

---

before beginning to search for meaning in his quest
for creating good script. Being up-to-date
with technological improvements was nice,
but the end product looked roughly the same.
Squiggly constricted lines of text without graceful loops.

The Palmer Method for learning to write had escaped him
in the second grade when he learned to draw letters
by moving the pen with his fingers rather than by moving his
arm. Learning to write with his left hand did not change the
shapes of the letters, as the brain controlled the product.
After reviewing his current skill level, he concluded
his longhand was as good as it was going to get.
An expensive writing instrument
would not change his style.

Being hopeful, there was a small place in his brain
cheering for the opportunity to master handwriting.
Pens such as the Rapidograph or the MontBlanc
beckoned him to take the plunge. Imagine
the advertisements: "Show the world you know
quality, and have the will to take a pen in hand,
placing your thoughts on paper for all to see."
Though the thoughts were impressive,
they did not equal legibility.
He concluded learning to type was his only option.

February 23, 2019

Endurance on the Mississippi River

We travel up and down
the Mississippi River
on a riverboat called *Endurance*.
Her engine purrs while she
cuts through the sliding water,
giving us an experience like no other.

The Mississippi's waters
are placid and smooth,
the sun is beating on the deck,
and I drowse, with sweat
running in my shirt
and dream of cool water and
foamy drinks.

The hour passes quickly.
And remembrance will paint
the pictures in beautiful strokes.

July 15, 2017

Seventy-Five

I woke up today
and found I was seventy-five.
I knew it was coming,
I have been following the schedule
for weeks.

You know, I have mixed
emotions about this.
Now, don't get me wrong,
I have no wish to be dead.
But there are certain infirmities
I could do without. I am like an old
steam engine. It takes awhile
to get me fired up.
An engine's boiler has to be hot
to generate the steam, plus
it has to stay hot to go anywhere.
There is no moving a cold engine by steam.

The steam engine train and I
go way back. When I was a kid.
No, let's be frank. Seventy years ago,
when the 8:15
from Omaha blew its whistle
coming round the curve,
the whistle's scream got me moving.
I had ten minutes to head for school.

So 'Old seventy-five' (that's me)
is stoked and ready to go,
nostalgia and all.

There is nobody alive
from my beginnings, so I have to say it:

Happy Birthday to me!

March 12, 2017

Catching Up

Returning from vacation
he was confronted with
the undone. At home,
he found a two-week
stack of mail, a depleted larder,
and a pile of dirty clothes.

His yard was a mess.
The garden teetered on
the brink of extinction,
while the yard displayed
triumphant weeds standing
tall in the yellowing grass.

At work he found
a huge pile of paper
on his desk, plus five hundred emails
on his computer, and any
problems he had before
he left, he still had.

His boss said, "Glad you're
back. We really need your input
on some major flare-ups that
occurred while you were gone.
By the way, did you have a good time?"

He began to contemplate
quantum physics,
idly wondering if he could be
in two places at once, and
what that would mean.
If he were identical in
both places, he would either
work or play. If he could split
oppositely then he could play

while he worked. Perhaps even
a three-way split would
be possible, work, work, play?

Starting to wonder
about independence and
influence, he began to feel
a developing headache.
Closing the drawer of his desk,
he headed for the door.
"Where are you going?" said his Boss.
"A short walk to run a quick experiment."
"Well hurry back, you need to catch up."

February 25, 2017

The Target Rifle

The case had been locked
for many long years.
Now, with the latches
thrown, and the lid pushed back,
a target rifle is exposed
resting on green velvet.

The handsome rifle
inspires awe and wonder
as it is gently removed from its case.
Now once again a shooter can savor
sending parcels of lead to a target's heart.

Coughing smoke, belching noise,
the rifle performs with great fanfare,
entertaining onlookers
during a bright afternoon.

And the old men
who remember all the days of war and peace
are content
to look, fondle, and pack it away.
As if its beauty and purpose
are too much for this time.

October 2, 2018

Velcro

I remember a world full of
buttons, bows, and zippers.
Then along came the hook
and loop fastener called Velcro,
asserting a new dimension
in clothing design and myriad
other uses.

Velcro is a little like human dating.
When two Velcro strips attach, it
is known as indeterminate matching,
compared to using a button, which is
determinate matching, or a marriage which
can be either.

Velcro was invented in 1941 by
a Swiss engineer. But it took
fifteen years to have a patented process,
and it was not widely used
in clothing until 1978. NASA was
an early adopter, using Velcro
for closures on space suits
and temporary attachments for tools
and other objects. But Velcro is not
a NASA invention.

In time, the familiar rip
of releasing Velcro
was heard everywhere,
a sound initially jarring,
faded into the world of white noise.
Velcro was great; it was
wonderful until it became a problem.

"What do you do when it stops working?
The hooks no longer grab the eyes and
convenience has fled the field.

Now you are stuck, the clothing
is not worn out, it just can't be worn."

"Well, what if you comb out the lint
with a wire brush?"

"It may help, but it is just as likely the hooks or
the eyes have failed. Now you
need a seamstress who is willing
to replace the non-gripping Velcro."

"Are you saying the world's greatest invention
can be a pain like anything else?"

"That may be, but it is not going away."

"It makes you wish for low technology.
Anybody can replace a button."

"If you have one."

April 19, 2017

The Symbiosis of Writers and Readers

The day came when I could no longer write.
But I could still read.
So I traveled the world
on the back of the written word.
I was never alone and
I experienced life in all its varieties.

In all my travels, near and far,
in times gone by, and in distant futures,
my itineraries were laid before me by the
generosity of writers.

I wrapped myself in their language
and I never wanted. But I wondered,
did they write for food, pleasure,
acknowledgement or from passion?
Whatever the reason, I lived
in their debt.

I knew that in a way I was fulfilling
their destiny. That I was part proof
of their purpose. And in that way,
I was paying them back, for as long
as I read, their thoughts lived on
and retained the possibility
of stimulating future readers to come.

December 13, 2017

Professional Dancers

Two couples were walking
the tunnel into the music hall,
when they spotted the ad for Move Beyond,
with Julianne and Derek Hough,
well-known dancers from Dancing with the Stars.

"Let's get tickets," started the journey
to the dance extravaganza. On arrival,
the hall was jammed with people,
and there was a disparity of men.

"Thirty women to one man,"
one man noted. "Is this a favorable ratio, or not?"
She said, "It only proves the
courage and sophistication of the men attending."
He replied, "I can get courage,
but I am not so sure about sophistication."

This generated discussion among the men.
"Is it courageous to listen to your wife,
or is it sophisticated?"
Said another, "It could be smart
and it could be prudent."

The first noting the number
of women without men remarked,
"It's a great time for women to grab a man for display,
sort of like arm-candy
in reverse."

Digging his hole deeper, he said,
"It gives the old girl a chance to display her catch,
show off how smart she is having a man on display,

and at the same time tweaking her sisters
who have nothing."

"Careful, said the other man,
You can generate a peck of trouble for us
if you are not careful."

"Do you mean it could be my last dance?"

June 10, 2017

They Never Had a Chance

Traveling approximately 20,000 miles
across the world for a once-in-a-lifetime visit
to Australia, they returned and
within twenty-five miles of home, one died
and the other was injured in a traffic accident.

Their car left the roadway, and funneled
by the topography of the ditch, struck
a rock berm placed across the ditch
as a water-control device. Becoming airborne,
the car flipped and landed
on its roof, killing the passenger
and injuring the driver.

The cause of the car leaving the roadway
is not clear. Time-zone stupor, an
inexperienced driver, mechanical failure
or something else, it did not matter.
The rock berm was a waiting death trap,
waiting for someone to run the slope
on the face of the berm
and fly to an uncertain future.

August 11, 2018

Cars

Today we looked at cars,
not just any of the
one point two billion cars
in the world. We picked two
of the population of cars
that run. There are others,
of course. Cars of beauty,
grace, and power,
cars carrying goods,
cars transporting people,
cars sitting abandoned that
used to run, cars junked in
bone-yards of steel,
and new cars that have yet to be
covered with lavish praise.

With cars, love is fickle;
and performance is expected and demanded.
And at times, their driver's hopes and dreams are fulfilled
before the long glide into rust.
But in general, cars are a cheat.
They almost never live up to expectations.

So we tried to determine their character.
After all, you pay them like prostitutes,
and you don't want to be left
standing on the roadside embracing yourself,
while other more faithful cars zip by in honking laughter.

In our looking, two looked trustworthy
and that is all we could expect.
Because, when we launch our choices
in the short years to come,
we will float the metal on concrete rivers,
attentive for malice, accidents, and disaster,
while hoping for pleasurable surprise.
For the day comes when you will not know who
to put out of their misery,
the driver or the car.

May 6, 2017

To Dream and Imagine

Humans have the capacity to dream
and imagine a potential future.
When pausing to rest or sleep
they begin to dream,
even before they are aware
of where they are. It is as if they are
beside a pool of dreams,
always available for browsing, reworking,
or sampling.

In sleep, dreams come unbidden
and are mostly forgotten.
But some are remembered
and are so vivid and attractive,
the dreamer begins
to think about creating
the vision as a living possibility.
Then voice and actions taken, alone,
or possibly with others,
empower the concept and begin
building the transition from plan to life.

With success, the dreamer becomes
a beacon for those who would align with
and take part in the concept of the dream.
The idea will remain active
until the dreamer's support disappears,
then the dream will be released,
perhaps to be picked up by another,
for dreams do not wear out.

December 11, 2018

The World of Learning

As a teenager I was aware of organizations
like the American Legion, the Veterans of
Foreign Wars, Quilting Societies, Bridge Clubs,
Dance Groups and various hobby groups.
I did not know much about them, except that
I was not eligible to be a part of them.

One outcome of being excluded from adult activities was
my friends and I would formulate our own groups
to be exclusionary, and we would have secret handshakes
and other nonsensical rules establishing membership requirements,
codes of conduct, and responsibilities.

These excursions into the world of adult groupings
had value in our development. Later when I participated
in professional societies, they provided a comfortable base
for being a member. They provided me an opportunity
to find my voice, and what I stood for in my chosen society.
I learned how to organize and keep a volunteer organization
moving forward. And later by elected leadership roles
I received training on being responsible for keeping
the local chapter functioning and in communication
with the parent society. All of these skills were valuable, and
transferable. And from this training and experience,
my whole life became fuller, leading me to be more effective
in my professional and civic duties.

August 28, 2019

Learning to March

I recently signed my life away
by joining the Army.
Now I am standing on a military parade ground
with my platoon. It is forty degrees Fahrenheit,
a light rain is falling, and it is getting dark.

My thoughts linger that we
will quit because of the weather.
The reality is, there is no chance.
The drill instructor seems to be waiting
for someone to complain.

At last it happened, we were standing at ease
and from the back came a voice:
"Sergeant, how long
do we have to be out here?"

"Until I am satisfied that
you know how to march!" He roared.

"We will march this parade ground flat.
We will march until you can stay in step.
We will march until you show me
you know how, or I am so sick
of your incompetence you will have
to carry me to the barracks.

"Platoon!" The Sergeant screamed.
"Attention!
Right face!
Forward march!"

And so we marched in close-order drill
for another hour. Then we marched to the barracks
and stood in the rain for mail call
before we were dismissed.

I had a hard choice, the mess hall closed
in ten minutes, I could have dry clothing
or immediate hot food? I chose food!

May 6, 2018

Cesspool

I am in a nightmare and I find myself
treading water in a governmental cesspool
created from mind-bending processes, rules, and laws.
I am looking at a passenger boat and it is sinking;
there is one life raft. I had hoped to get out of the water,
but the crew is throwing people overboard. Then
I watch the crew assault each other until only one is left and
the bodies have been pushed aside. The 'survivor' sees me,
paddles over and asks
if I would like to join him.

As I consider the offer, I think back and
remember a friend who asserted that laws were enacted
to regulate the slobs. It seems things are reversed.
Governmental agencies acting as slobs develop rules
that are oppressive. Government should serve the people;
for instance, under the Department of Education,
where is the educational curriculum that would truly facilitate
people becoming successful? Where is the promised land
of opportunity for all, but especially those
who are becoming adults?

Does one beat-up thug in the life raft offer solutions,
or platitudes and nostrums? I think about the crew
on the sinking boat as an example of governmental
regulators. Did they realize what was needed
to keep it running and afloat? Did they take charge
of the health and well-being of the passengers?
Or did they treat them with contempt for being part
of the great unwashed?

For an individual becoming successful, it is fair to say,
if no one shows you the way, then you have to figure it out.
And you need an economy in which to survive while
you grow your skill set. A decent economy used to be available.
I remember it. I worked in it. And I ended up
in government working the processes regulating transportation

projects, interpreting the rules, watching them grow in number and complexity every year while looking for common-sense solutions in the regulation of projects.

As the population grows, the needs grow, especially for the needs of tolerance and respect. But those are hard to come by when the economy and education needed to function are missing. Is it any wonder we are ruled by cynicism? People without jobs, or a trajectory into economic well-being, are grasping for straws. They also vote, and some of those votes will go to the perpetrators of our sorrows. Others will go to empty promises, and still others will go to people who care about the country and are working to move it forward.

In summation, "God help us all." Our economy is declining rapidly for those without the flexibility to shift their work skills as more and more governmental efforts backfire and make working conditions less efficient, and more and more people are unable to work. Anarchy beckons. Do I slip below the surface wondering how it all turns out? Or do I join the fray on the lifeboat to better my circumstances?

March 6, 2016

Confusion Reigns

One night, we hosted
old folks for dinner.
We drank a lot of wine
and we talked
the whole night through,
mostly common stuff,
but some regarding an imperfect future.

"It is time for us to look for
what may come," said one.
Avoiding the new tack, another said,
"We are nearly out of wine."
He pointed to the future
of an empty wine bottle
causing the conversation
to jolt to a halt in the present.
Suddenly, they realized
the evening had passed by.

The next day their cars met
in the middle of the street, and
as in small towns everywhere,
they stopped for a chat with windows down.
After called greetings, one inquired about
the imperfect future mentioned the night before.
Without the support of wine,
no one wanted to speak.

It seemed one was mumbling and lost in the last century,
one was clearly wandering in the sands of time,
and one was putting her grave as the new.
With the group's focus so imperfect and bizarre,
they muttered *adieus*
and drove away.

June 10, 2017

GREG P. BUSACKER

The Land Keeps its Secrets:
A Tale of Two Who Passed This Way

You can find two site markers
on a farm in Wisconsin,
where the land hosts the souls
of a man and his wife,
who found peace thereby.

One site marker is an inscribed stone slab
mounted at the peak of a grouted cairn,
lying deep in the woods, near a stream
in a small grotto.

The simple inscription marks the passing
of an introspective successful man.
Possessed with a towering intellect
and demanding self-expression.
He was an enigma to some,
a mentor to many,
and loved and respected
in the business community.

Markers at a second site
are located one quarter mile away
overlooking a shallow valley.
There, two artistic sculptures
of sandhill cranes express
a woman's dance of life
as a self-expression between
her family and her businesses.
The birds also call forth her spirit,
for like her husband, she was
a woman of vision,
and an expressive risk taker
in business.

When the couple came to the farm,
it was a reward for a life well lived.
They left the farm as free spirits

with only the memorial sites
to note their passing.

Today, those seeing the markers
may wonder about the story behind them,
but they will little note the impacts
the couple had on the land
and the legacy they left.
For the land keeps its secrets
and only the most obvious
are available to those who travel by.

February 5, 2017

Seventy-Seven

Seventy-seven
has a way off rolling
off of the tongue.
And each year's birthday
celebration has a
little more gravity
added to the event.

There is an uncertainty
of continuance present,
and the possibility
of a major illness lingers.

Thinking of the whole,
there is no doubt
that I am in the
fourth quarter
of my life. And when
I write these evaluative
briefs, they always cause
wonderment in my day.

The energy left over
after chores, medical
appointments, and the frequent
"have-to-do-this-now"
is often insufficient
for fun, hobbies, reading and
community activities.

But, so what?"
Every day becomes a celebration
of another step in life.
Happily, seventy-seven
resonates for me.

March 16, 2019

My Frustrations with the U.S. Congress

The United States Congress is the nation's
most exclusive club. There are 435 members
in the House of Representatives, 100 members
in the Senate, and six nonvoting members.

Members of the House are to represent
the people's concerns in a state's Congressional Districts
based on population. Only two Senators represent
an entire state, irrespective of the states' population.
While a state's representation may be unequal between
the House and Senate, this representation has nothing
to do with people's general opinions. The entire U.S.
Congressional membership is often categorized
(by the people they represent) as a pool of liars.

Most members of Congress are elected
from individuals who have served government
at the local and state levels, but some are appointed.
Many have decided they could do more for their neighbors
and the country by serving at the national level.
There are also many who think they could do more
for themselves by being at the national level,
where there is a river of money available for influence.

Individuals who go through the election process
hone their skills in communication and presentation.
They become quite good at appearing to be
articulate, honorable, and truthful. The operative
word here is "appearing," which becomes
the basis for assertions regarding what they will do,
and what they stand for.

The populace often complains of not having
representation. But based on the two-party system,
at any one time and on any issue, about one half
of the populace will feel represented and one half not.
Their most common complaint arises from dealing
with professional liars.

GREG P. BUSACKER

Those who are elected to this most exclusive club
are skilled in all forms of dissembling untruthfulness, including
lying, avoiding the question, using nuance, and failing to keep
promises. Simple statements of fact are seldom heard, unless it
is a negative description of the opposition.

Evaluating the process, many wags will say:
- When you vote for a new or returning liar, what do
  you expect?
- If all your choices are professional liars, how do you
  avoid despair?
- Do you discuss how it should be different?
- Do you campaign for the liar with whom you feel the
  most comfort?

There appears to be a comfort level in the individual voter
for a certain degree of larceny in representation.
Could it be the U.S. Congress does represent the people?
Or is corruption and malfeasance so difficult to prosecute,
the individual voter feels helpless?

Often the voter has to choose between two bad choices.
And as a further insult, it seems the Club is adept at
protecting their own. New candidates are at a considerable
disadvantage when running against an incumbent.
It seems we are devolving into a third-world experience of
governance.

October 1, 2017

Doing Taxes

It's the IRS you see,
the giant Federal Agency
controlling the fate of millions
with complex rules,
fitting their whims of: "Send it in."

Rules created by lawyers,
vague, and confusing:
a language all its own,
using English words to
give foreign meaning
to a sea of pain.

Facing taxes,
you launch your boat,
you must row to avoid
the whirlpools of deceit,
dead ends and enticing chutes.

Uttering fervent prayers
you try to get there,
you set time aside
and do your taxes, stopping only
to wax philosophically
about this wretched fate.

But looking, you'd think
one doesn't mind
the horrid waste of time,
and good money badly spent.

It's all an act, of course:
inauthentic cheerfulness,
to turn away the threat
of wearing prison garb
during your single daily hour
in the yard.

September 29, 2016

The Ranch Pickup

They called it a ranch pickup,
nothing to do with women,
it is just an old beat-up truck.
It came to be in its new home forty years ago
with 129,000 miles logged by someone else.
Now with 300,000 miles, there is hardly an original part.

The rancher was remembering
and taking inventory of the pickup
as the tractor dragged it over
to a weak corner of the corral that needed shoring.
"You deserve better than this," he thought,
"but the cattle are coming to the yard
and loading the cattle trucks will start soon."

The ranch pickup used to be blue,
now patches of white show through the gray.
The dents in the door were caused by cattle gates,
cattle, and the occasional deer.
The frame used to be straight,
but that was before it hauled 40,000 tons
of feed over two track roads and back pastures.
The alignment didn't bother the tires.
Sand may be abrasive, but it is soft and yielding
in a road bed.

The windshield is cracked and gravel-chipped,
the mirrors and horn are a distant memory.
Shock absorbers are remembered by the pain in your butt.
The steering is loose and the truck weaves like a drunk.
It has a standard shift on the floor and you used
to turn the hubs for four-wheel drive.
Now it is four-wheel drive all the time because
cowboys don't like to walk.

The outside door latches are broken
and the driver's window is permanently down

so you can reach in and open the door,
as well as spit tobacco juice while driving.
The springs in the seat are covered by an old gunnysack.
The ignition key is lost and hanging wires under the dash
are twisted together to start and run the engine.

The only switch working on the dash runs
a siren installed to call the cattle to feed.
The radio dial is stuck on bad cattle prices and sad music.
The dash is protected by mismatched gloves,
unpaid bills and vaccine syringes, plus cans
of Copenhagen in summer and Skoal in winter.
A 30/30 rifle rides the gun rack in the back window.
An old lasso rope hooks the empty pegs. There is always
a whisky bottle under the seat, and a rubber overshoe
is being used as a toolbox.

The bed of the truck no longer holds
beer cans, small tools, scraps of barbed wire
or small items. The muffler and the truck
parted ways in 1999. The engine uses oil
but in the house yard, oil smoke keeps the flies
and the mosquitos at bay.

The suspension was lost while roping sick calves
and occasional coyotes in rugged pastures.
The tires are of odd sizes, including one white wall from 1950.
Originally it had two headlights; now it has one,
and an old rag for a gas cap.
But even in retirement the truck is still useful,
storing whatever will fit in the bed and cab.

The truck is a legacy of pain fueled by sex,
humor, and the suffering of others.
But its biggest problem is a teenage girl
wanting to drive it to school.

Greg Busacker and Marvin Cox
August 24, 2017
Previously published in *The Hooker County Tribune*. Used with permission.

The Gifts of Naming and Booking

After a long look, the Professor
awarded the newly minted Poet
a new book.

Said the Professor:
"I have given you
this book as a symbol of
who you have become.
I've had the pleasure of watching
you grow. And if I take poetic license,
it is time for you to discover who you are
and what you have become for all to see.
We pray your writings continue to delight
for you stand before me named Poet."

The Poet replied:
"I share your wonder. You
have been my mentor in
this journey and have caused me
to plumb the depths of my emotions
to write with feeling and joy.
This book shall be my tiller
as I cast off in my boat named
Thank You.

"I have been entrusted
with your gift and I shall
endeavor to sail the seas
describing the world
as I have seen it, knowing
my art lies in the unseen depths
below my feet, for I have become
a fisherman of words.

"Should I become lost,
this worldly book has the power
to call me back by trueing

my course. In Missouri
we say, 'Show Me,' and you
have done so. You have
my thanks and my heart."

December 26, 2016

Book Talk

While giving an oral presentation of his work,
his emotional response to many
of his poems caused his voice to crack.
Even though he had read his poems aloud
countless times, the emotional displays
distressed him.

Later during lunch, the suppressed emotions
boiled to the surface, the pain and the loss
were palpable, reminding him that his family
was now a memory and beyond interaction.

As he reviewed the talk and his reactions,
he saw what he had done with his writing.
He had poured his anguish, his love,
and his fear into the poems, so that the reader
could find similar emotions in their own lives.

He had known a loss of self-control
was always possible
when reading his poetry aloud.
Still, he was surprised by his delayed reactions
and the power of his words.

July 8, 2018

Hockey at the Lake House

Ice Hockey on a Missouri lake
is a rarity. The game was to
start at noon. Players had been
dribbling in for the last hour. But some
had never left from the night before.

Nobody was moving fast,
and donning ice skates did
not seem to help. The lake was
frozen and the so-called rink
was set up parallel to the dam.
The only reason for the placement
was to control the recovery of the puck
after a shot on goal. In other words,
the lake was longer than wide.

Gabe (The Mountain) had taped
old *Look* magazines around his legs,
and old phone books over his shins.
The other goal would to be manned by guts
and a prayer. The goalie was still numbed
from last night's drinking, and he seemed
not to notice his body was going to be
sacrificed.

Finally, ten players made it
to the ice. And the game began.
The first shot on goal was stopped
by Gabe and the yellow pages. The
puck was shuttled out to a defense man
and she blazed down the ice, side-stepped
a defender deked the goaltender and scored.

The celebration was short-lived as
most of the players tried to regain breath
while they were downing a beer. Later, the

GREG P. BUSACKER

unprotected goalie took a puck on the thigh
and dropped like a stone, saving a goal,
but putting him out of the game. Gabe suffered
no such injury and managed to shut out the opposition.

Two hours later, when the assembled players were
gassed and lying on the bank of the lake,
the onlookers began to feel it was safe to be on the ice.
The only sounds were from scattered laughter
and belching from prostrate players lying on the bank.
Somebody said, "Who the hell came up with this idea?"
Nobody knew for sure, but next weekend sounded good
for another game. And if it stayed cold enough for safe-ice
they would have another go at Missouri Hockey.

Greg Busacker & Chuck Esterley

Winter, 2019

IN THE BEST OF COMPANY

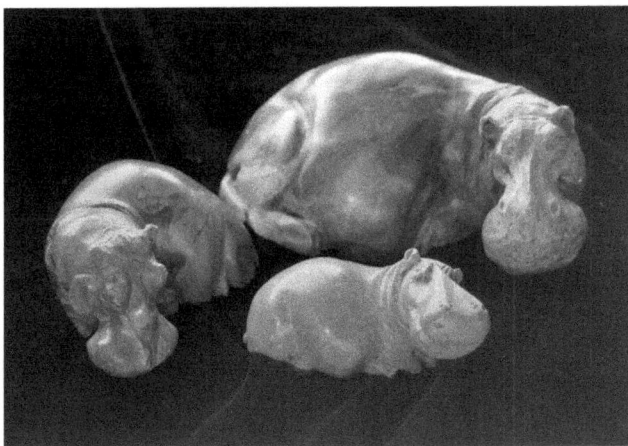

Thanksgiving: It's an Old Story

They were a divergent group
with tendrils of relationships
reaching back decades and centuries.
Most were from the known world
with a few anomalies.

They came together
from near and far
at a time of celebration
in a place offered for the gathering.
Most came willingly
in anticipation. Some were
reluctant and a few were hostile,
but they came.

As they trickled in
a mountain of food
began to grow; food
an offering to all, with
favorite recipes representing
the melding of families.

As all were welcome
the day passed in
comfort, with food and drink
lubricating social interactions
across the generations.

At day's end,
all grew thankful for
the day and for the love
that was present. On the way
home, they planned for the
coming year in anticipation
of the next gathering.
After all, it is an old and
satisfying story.

November 25, 2016

Cold Beer: A Tragedy Averted

In the bathroom at night
while waiting for early light,
his tranquility was wrought
by a sobering thought.

What has happened to the beer?

A favorite brew
rarely available
was stashed in a car
now parked in the snow
where ice would grow.

Ice expanding the beer,
the bottles would break,
the beer would be a waste;
and I'd get nary a taste.

Worse, as time passed
my wife would ask,
"Honey, why does the car
smell of stale beer?"
l would have to admit
that I knew why.

So I strode to the phone.
Checking the weather,
the numbers flash by:
38° Fahrenheit just now,
dropping to 20° by 6:00 AM.
By golly, there was still time for a fix.

As I rushed to the door,
the temperature dropped more.
When I crossed the parking lot,
it was 13° above zero and snowing.

Going to the frozen car,
I opened the door and reached in for six.
Then ran back to the room like Saint Nick.

Standing in the beer's golden light, I was jubilant.
The beer was in great shape.
Tragedy had been averted that date.

January 12, 2018

Remembering My Heritage at Christmas

It is Christmas and the house
seems empty except for me.
A tree is needed to bear
the weight of my memories.

The lower boughs to hold our
grandparents bold,
solid German stock of old.
And they give rise to our parents
circling the tree with spirals of brilliant light.

Joining the parents are the many
aunts and uncles with lights
of red and green. Shining ornaments
display the numerous cousins.
Brothers and sisters get special lights
as we decorate the tree this night.

Tinsel strands stand for friends and
they cover the tree with a shimmering
cloak. Finally, to top the tree, our daughter,
the angel. All a reminder of the gifts
of heritage and the love of family.
For we are truly blessed this Christmas.

December 25, 2016

Christmas Greeting

Words alone cannot convey
what you are to us this day.

You do us honor at every dinner date
and we strive to not be late.

Conversations range wide and true;
but in the end, they point to our love for you.

So until we meet at our frequent fete;
we wish you a Merry Christmas
and a Joyous New Year.

May they be filled with
love and affection.

December 8, 2016

Dad and Pedro Take a Nap

I was reading an old letter
my father wrote
where he talked about
our dog named Pedro.

According to Dad,
he was taking a nap
with Pedro stomping
around on the bed
looking for a place
to lay his head.

Searching for satisfaction,
trying this place and that,
finally down at Dad's side
with his front feet
over Dad's shoulder,
cheek to cheek, together they lay.

Pedro fell into a snoring slumber.
How Dad slept he didn't say.
But you can bet
Mother was away.

January 14, 2017

Today is Your Birthday

My love,
today is your Birthday.
Your birth happened
and I was unaware.
But when I first saw you
I became aware
of you.

You are the love of my life,
my best friend.
I marvel at your skills
in supporting other people.
You have wonderful friends
and your family
has always been my family.

Happy Birthday lover,
may we experience many more.
I Love You.

Greg

December 17, 2015

Always on December Seventeenth

You know,
I never counted on this.
Always, I lived as if
I would live a long life;
that I would outlive
nearly all my loved ones.

I did not want the role
of a tragic death, and
it may not happen. But
I want you to know
I never wanted it.

I will take what
I get, and live
with grace and power,
being who I can be
for those around me.

For you my love,
worry not, for my
strength is built on
your love for me.
And should you pass
before me, it will
carry me through.

Our life together
has turned into a miracle.
And miracles have a way
of hanging around for centuries.

So I will count on it always
being your birthday on
December seventeenth.

So "Happy Birthday
my sweet, number 70 is here."

December 12, 2017

A Family Gathering at Christmas

The holiday of Christmas is well marked
on the calendar. The celebration is complex,
a mixture of emotions, religious expressions,
travel, obligations, gift giving, food, and enjoyment.

Everyone has a role to play, whether they are
at the central gathering or not. It is actually
an accepted cultural excuse to be home, and
an opportunity to be with people you don't particularly like.

The splendor of decorations, presents, and
multiple food preparations made once a year take center stage
where wide-eyed little kids and big-eyed adults
try to see how much they can eat.

In preparations, houses are cleaned
until they squeak. Special clothing, drinks,
and music set an amazing table feast
for eyes and ears.

July 1, 2019

Best Buddies

Best buddies since age four.
How could one ask for more?
They carry more weight than before,
but the link is still there
and they really don't care.

Reuniting, they talk
about their news
and as descriptions go by,
the other will cry,
"Why didn't I know this?"

If they talked every day,
much they would say.
But when they try
to sync their lives in an afternoon,
including changes over time,
it is too hard to address. So
they do their best
and forget the rest.

They talk about weight,
how less would be great.
They talk about doctors,
like they were life's proctors.
They talk and they read;
it is all that they need,
and they bask in old love
that fits like a glove.

Now at age seventy,
the years have flown by
in the blinks of their eyes
and they yearn for the future
for there is much to explore;
more frequent reunions
nicely fill the clamor for more.

GREG P. BUSACKER

But be as it may,
they've had quite a day,
and whatever the morrow may bring
best buddies will choose the right thing.

October 9, 2017

A Tribute to Garrett

I once met a man
with seemingly
boundless energy.
His enthusiasm was contagious.
Even if you knew
you could not duplicate his actions,
you wanted to try.

I watched people
he was training and I knew
if he were working with me,
he would integrate my frailties
into meaningful actions.
Eventually, I did sign on;
I never regretted having done so.

Garrett is the man,
and the stockings he wears
on Fridays will be missed by us
but enjoyed by others as he moves on,
attentive to his family
and his new charges
in physical fitness.

Garrett, thank you
for your love and appreciation!

We wish you well!

May 18, 2019

These Men are My Brothers

I

Marksmanship is a little-known intercollegiate sport.
At the University of Nebraska, the rifle team
was supported as a Club Sport by the University and
by the Reserve Officers' Training Corps (ROTC). Each year
the Rifle Team was formed from about fifteen shooters,
with ten being selected for the first and second teams.
Competitions were held on Campus and with other teams, with
ROTC programs in Conference and Non-Conference Schools.
From about 1958 to 1964, seven individual members
of the University Rifle Team became close friends. Meeting in a
basement apartment, they didn't realize that the dirty songs,
jokes, and beer would forge the bonds of life long friendships.
They were just having a good time. It developed into something
much more important and enduring. The bond was so close, they
considered each other life-time brothers. They continued to interact
through a broad spectrum of outdoor activities after graduating.

II

On Friday, one of six brothers I gained
on joining the Rifle Team came to town.
I was pleased to see him, as we were driving to compete
in an annual rifle match. We had some planning to do
to firm up the group's annual get-together.
Over the years, the group has become a family
composed of team members plus their spouses.
The group has been remarkably stable,
losing one team member ten years ago,
and one spouse eighteen months ago.

Our relationships within the group are strong.
We rely on each other, each providing something for another.
All of us have overlapping skills in fishing, hunting, and shooting.
We love and respect our wives.
They are our partners in supporting field trips,
such as hunting and other social interactions.
Around 1980, gone from the University for nearly twenty years,
it was suggested we get together for a fall pheasant hunt.

We had so much fun,
we repeated the fall bird hunts for the next thirty years.

III

Much specialized knowledge serves as a backdrop for our
relationships. These are the things guys do together
and relationships expand and strengthen along the way
in the doing. All our talents are shared and a strong synergy
grows when we get together. New ideas arising from activities
are able to bend and mold for examination without much ridicule.

Our time together is filled with activities
in preparation for activities related to hunting and fishing.
Working professions include a chemist, a skilled machinist,
a surveyor, civil engineer, cattle rancher, teacher, an attorney, and
a natural resource specialist. Conversation stems from
knowing specialized and arcane information. Mutual and shared
hobbies include a knowledge of literature, poetry,
brewing beer and wine, and sufficient carpentry
skills to build smaller structures.

U.S. Army Military Service produced one fixed-wing pilot,
a helicopter mechanic, a Paratrooper in the 101st Airborne,
one Specialist 5th Class, three First Lieutenants and one
Major of the U.S. Army; two served in Viet Nam.
We are fortunate and proud to be brothers.

November 4, 2016

GREG P. BUSACKER

I Don't Know

I
"I don't know," seems
an innocuous phrase,
often uttered with regret,
for if the speaker knew the answer,
then things would be all right.

It starts at an early age, when you
may not understand the language
conveying the question. But it can be
truthful and merely the foundation
of your knowledge. Or it can be a lie
that's used in response to: "Who did this?!"
Then it is a dodge to escape punishment
or to protect a playmate.

II
As you age, it becomes a black mark
not to know. You would rather lie
than appear ignorant, hoping others will be satisfied
and leave you alone.

If one is being avidly questioned by interrogators,
"I don't know" is not considered an acceptable answer.

Interrogator A: "You must know something, some bit
of information that will be key
in understanding the issue."

It takes nerve to say, "I don't know,"
because the phrase becomes a stopping point.

Interrogator B: "No need to go any further, he doesn't
know."

Interrogator A: "Maybe, maybe not. He could be lying,
he could be stupid, or he doesn't like us,
and he is not going to be of help."

You can almost hear thoughts of torture
to get to the truth of the matter.

III

Later in life, you are supposed to know
and you may not. But you know the limits
of your knowledge and if you cannot give
a complete answer, you can do some research
on the issue and report back. The phrase becomes:
"I don't know, but I will find out." Now it is not
a stopping point; it causes a delay and it may
come to pass that the questioner will be satisfied.

IV

When the phrase is a true expression
of your lack of knowledge,
there is power in saying "I don't know."
Particularly when you are dealing with suppositions
about what happened, motives, and hearsay.
You are on solid ground to say:
"The events are a mystery to me; I was not there."

December 4, 2018

Wake Up

By the light of early morning,
my fingers are skimming
the surface of my sleeping mate.
Skin, hair, fabric, it is all the same.

Suddenly reacting she roars,
"Leave me be."

I say, "It's time."

Then she pleads, "Just ten more minutes."

Ah, the refrain of a lifetime.
But daylight is burning,
so the fingers go back to work,
nimbly avoiding the slashing hand.

"Leave me be," she bellows.

I repeat myself, "Very well, but I'll be back."

The next skirmish is more carefully planned.
Fresh coffee as bait,
a reminder of the time,
And if all else fails, turning loose the dogs.

June 30, 2019

Memories of The Rock

On behalf of the University of Nebraska Rifle Team

Everybody has a story about our friend "The Rock."
He had improbable skills with a rifle, a shotgun and a fishing pole.
Or, throw in a bow and arrow, a crossbow and fishing with an
unbaited hook, then you begin to scratch the surface.

The Dr. Doolittle of the hunting world,
The Rock called the animals to him year after year,
and large and small, they fell into his cooking pot.
Their haunts and habits were second nature to him and
it did not matter if they had hair, fur, scales, or feathers,
The Rock was a hunter and he would have survived
in any habitat known to man.

In the human world, he was a man of uncommon generosity.
His roles of husband, father, teacher, and friend were seamless.
He always had time for fun, laughter and hard work.

His bonds with the University of Nebraska Rifle Team ran deep.
In later years the pheasant hunt was the glue for the call
to drive hundreds of miles to be together once more.
We took the opportunity to hunt, talk, and walk the autumn fields
shooting a bird or two by day and shooting the bull by night.

The Rock wore his nickname at a young age.
And for over fifty years he was our rock.
He is missed by family and friends but he
remains in our stories and memories
as an uncommon man, and all we could hope to be.

August, 2010

GREG P. BUSACKER

TENDER AFFECTIONS

TENDER AFFECTIONS

Things Happen

His wife told him,
"You are going to write about it."

"Why?" the man said.

She replied, "Because that is what you do."

So he sat, and he wrote.
And it was like everything he had ever read
was available at his fingertips.

Countless words in unbelievable
configurations and assemblages appeared.
Stories came to him, and as he wrote
he weaved in his experiences and his dreams.

And those who read his writings
were moved to step away
from the ordinary and begin fulfilling
the dreams lurking in the corners of their minds.

It seemed trite for the man to say
to people at large, "You can do it."

And people would ask, "How can I do this?"
It was a question they had been asking all
their lives when confronted with a new task.
But once they abandoned
whatever had been stopping them,
their lives were never the same again;
they became fully integrated with the lives of
their families and their communities.
All because "things happen" and some people take action.

November 4, 2018

The Oath of Care and Love

When we were young
we swore an oath
to care for one another
in sickness and in health.
Little did we know
how we would be engaged
under our promise,
and all I know is we step forward
to answer the call when it comes.

Sometimes it is a few days,
or at worst a month or two,
such as when you had your double bypass,
or when I was dizzy. But this time
it is indeterminate, and still
you step forward to take on the demands,
not knowing how it will go,
keeping track of my medications,
living with constant concerns,
trying to ensure I listen to my body and to you.

Our health is a partnership.
You remember because
I am the evidence you see all the time
while I struggle to be present to do
what I need to do. When you look
at me, I may be in denial,
in resistance, or in need.

It is clear to me,
my everyday progress
is sheltered by your umbrella.
You have my love and my gratitude,
and you have my permission to remind me
that you have my permission,
to tell me what I need to do.

GREG P. BUSACKER

I swear to you, I will have the grace
to listen and execute your desires.
So help me God.

May 30, 2018

Wherever I Go, There Is Family

A long time ago,
I arrived in Duluth, Minnesota at the end of June.
The lilacs were just blooming by the lake.
Duluth springtime development
was a month behind Southern Minnesota
and I was amazed. The local weatherman always
remarked, it will be cooler or warmer
by the lake depending on the season.
At the time, I had no comprehension of the impact
of Lake Superior on the local weather.

I lived in a small camper trailer
in the campground at Knife River, Minnesota.
Helen Meriam was the owner and we became friends.
The camper was small. I could lie in the bunk,
or sit at the table,
but I could not stand up.
I cooked eggs for breakfast,
made my lunch and ate elsewhere for all other meals,
mostly at the Sky Line Café.

I was conducting a research project
as a guest worker in the Environmental Protection
Administration (EPA) Laboratory.
As it happened, I was directed to see Gary Phipps
for direction on setting up fish tanks
and the needed equipment. Gary Holcombe
came with Gary Phipps as they were inseparable office mates.
I worked closely with them and received invaluable help.

Sometime in August, Gary Phipps invited me
to stop over for dinner at their house in Two Harbors.
There I met his wife, Bonnie and their three kids, Tim, Amy, and Paul.
Jonathan came along much later.
They rapidly assimilated me into the family.
I watched "Hill Street Blues" and helped the kids
with their homework. I made the effort
to see my wife Carol in Saint Paul every weekend,

and often gave Bonnie a ride to the Twin Cities
where she would visit her dad, or her brothers.
All of my family members met the Phipps family
at one time or another.

Bonnie is one of the most gregarious
people I have ever met. She knew
nearly everybody, or knew someone that they
knew—sometimes once or twice removed.
Gary was a solid friend; he did not talk a lot,
and he was someone I was comfortable with
even when he was not talking.
He was skilled in building and fixing nearly
everything. I marveled at his capacities.
He did his best to provide for the family.
He loved to hunt and fish, and made
some incredible fishing treks into the Boundary Waters.

The family was very religious and I was not,
but their Christian spirit accepted me
and I never felt any pressure or criticism of
my own spirituality. I think they were and are
the model for Christian generosity.

The research project lasted ten months.
My interactions with the Phipps' family have now been
going on thirty-three years. When we moved from
Minnesota, distance put its usual crimp on being
in contact. Gary passed on in the late spring of
this year. I feel his death as a personal tragedy.
I have tried to detail the importance
of Gary's generosity in sharing himself and his
family with me. But I do not think I can do it
justice. I do know my life has been enriched
and expanded because of the Phipps family,
and I am part of it.

September 2, 2017

Entreaty

I

Julie, you send me running,
into my library deep
searching for a poem to keep.

A poem to share,
so you may read my emotions;
as if my thoughts of you
and my words are not enough.

After searching with care
I found my library bare.
And rather than saying *adieu*
my pen will have to do.

II

You may question what you see in me
with nothing apparent for you,
but beneath the surface
lies a commitment made to you.

For I say,
"The love is true and deep,
freely given and yours to keep.

So approach my vision,
setting aside your suspicions
and reach to find my rendition.

A choice I so hope you take,
but one for you I cannot make."

May 17, 2014

A New Son

In my voice as a father

In March of a year
in the early 1940s,
I met my new son
in Saint Louis. I was
seven days short
of my twenty-seventh birthday,
and my dear wife who
had helped raise her
seven siblings, now
had one of her own.

Not that she had
a free ride with this one.
He was a big baby
at eight pounds, and
the nurses named him
Bosco. We had our work
cut out for us.

Outside, the world was at war.
Everything was uncertain.
I had been rejected
for pilot training because
of my eyesight. Now,
my child and my profession
have cemented me into Saint Louis
for the duration of the war.
Thank god there is no fighting here.

March 29, 2018

I Did Not Know You Were a Poem

As he handed his six-year-old granddaughter
a book of poetry he had written,
she said, "Oh! I did not know
you were a poem."

"I am," he replied. "And I keep it
well hidden too. But what sort
of poem would you like me to be?"

"I don't know," she replied. "We have a poetry class
at school, but it seems complicated."

"Not necessarily so," he said. "Around you,
I am a poem of love and admiration."

>   My daughter's daughter
>   Easy to love and admire
>   A beautiful girl

"I can also be one of happiness and gratitude
for who you are."

>   Happy day today
>   I am grateful to be alive
>   With you at my side

"I can be a poem of grief and sadness."

>   My soul needs a jump
>   Our dog died, her love is lost
>   And I feel empty

"Or, I can be one of life and joy."

>   Feel a cool fall wind
>   The air is dry, the season changing
>   Leaves waiting on trees

To fly on the wind
A summer spent developing
Now waiting to launch

"I can be a poem of many things,
but I cannot be one of hate
or war when I am with you."

"I think I would like you to be just you," she said.

"Well," he said, "since in part we reflect each other,
let us take what pleases us so we can enjoy
being with each other. We can carry forth
our love and respect. Remember, I am the created poem
you requested and you are poetry yourself.
Both will come to life again when we next meet."

"WOW," she said.

September 6, 2017

Writing for Life

Alex remembered the D,
earned by turning in religious dogma.
The original assignment had been to write
a paragraph or two about something known.

At first, thinking there was
nothing to write about, confusion set in.
But then religion came to mind.
After all, his young life included
years of going to church.
However, he really had not been
paying attention.

Finding some religious writing in
an encyclopedia that looked good,
and after copying a few paragraphs,
the assignment was submitted.
The returned paper came back
marked D. Seeing the mark,
divine came to his mind, plus two
additional descriptors: drivel and dolt.

Not wanting to, but needing to, Alex asked, "Why a D?"

"I asked for your writing, not someone else's.
Use the limited imagination available to you
and write a descriptive paragraph of what
you do, or what you saw and what you
think about it."

This encounter had been
in his first quarter of life.
And taking the teacher's comments
seriously, he began to work on writing,
finding his own ideas were good,
but the presentations were poor.

Eventually, after constructing
cohesive paragraphs, his papers began
to receive decent marks.

By the third quarter of his life,
he was writing professionally and
wholly interested in communicating clearly
with his readers.

Years later in the fourth quarter
of living, while writing about
the edges of his life,
he found himself suspended above an abyss
where the power of his words
generated the supporting currents beneath him,
and by the grace of the supporting air,
his unique perspectives on life and living
became available to his readers.

It was clear he was writing for life.
For, were he to stop writing,
both Alex and the expression of his being
would disappear into the abyss below.

April 23, 2017

Difficult Choices

Are
you able
to define
a time
when
you became
a captive audience?

Were
you
being held
by your
spouse
to talk
about choices
you were
avoiding?

Did
you find
yourself
trapped
while driving
in a car?
At the wheel
you
were running
but
not hiding.

Perhaps
it was
at the
table
where you
were able
to eat,
but
the talk
was unavoidable.

Since a meal
was
not enough
to ring you in;
you fled
across country.

The relentless
pursuit
seemed
unfocused,
yet
you were
expertly herded
into
the box canyon.

The canyon
had
been inviting
and
interesting.
But it
was found to have
high
vertical walls
and….

No Exit.

The game was over.

She said, "Now choose!"

August 22, 2018

Seventy-Six

You know, I will be seventy-six in fourteen days.
As you may remember, in the last few years,
I have written a new ditty each year addressing
how I feel about all of this.

To reiterate, I have a wonderful wife and
I am the luckiest of men because
I would not be writing this without her; I would be dead.
I have written extensively regarding my love for her
and I can write more, but it is enough for the moment
to acknowledge what she brings to the table.
For, I am I and she is she, and it is certain
we are each more because of the other.

So how do I feel about being seventy-six?
I have always romanticized the year
of the Declaration of Independence.
As it happens, the seventeen is long gone by,
but I get to celebrate seventy-six every day of the coming year.
This seems a plus!

Outside my window stands my barking dog.
She wants attention and does this every day.
As a mild irritant she reminds me of the times
when I do not walk as freely as I once had.
I must admit no one else seems to mind,
and at times, I join them.

Other than that, the body is working as well as
or better than one might hope.
I do pretty much what I want to do.
And I look forward to the coming year,
surrounded by people I know and love,
with the expectation of adding to the circle.
What more could I ask?

February 28, 2018

The Endurance of Love

Thinking a retrospective on love was appropriate,
he went on a long drive on his seventy-sixth Birthday.
Reflecting on the times he was aware
he was loved, versus the times he thought
he was not. He concluded the periods where love
was present far exceeded the times he thought love absent.

He noted the mix of his companions
changed with the presence of love.
It seemed the gatherings were a reflection of love's focal point.
Ranging from one person to another,
or to something else, like a person to alcohol,
or misery to miserable.

The years when he struggled
seemed to have passed slowly, while
years in the cocoon of love
blazed by so quickly he wondered
if he was overlooking something.

He found that advice on love
was always available. But
being responsible for the presence
of love was rarely mentioned.

Arriving home, he realized love evolves with the acts
of giving and receiving to and from others.
And love endures as an act of mutual generosity
with each person sharing responsibility for love's presence.

May 19, 2018

The Sprite of Wonder and Light

You came into my life
to my wonder and delight.
And for twenty-five years
I have been the luckiest of men.

In our first meeting a promise
was made and I was afraid,
but I jumped into a void
black as the night.

Drifting softly with only
my voice and my pen,
I found you were the Sprite
illuminating the night, and
I could see far beyond me.

We built slowly
a word at a time
in a place where we
watched our world expand
to our love and our joy.

We each received
something different:
for me, a daughter and a wife
whole and complete; for you,
answers to questions of old,
plus the power to be bold.

Receiving love
from more sources,
you could see what you had,
and not what you'd lost.
Now as you direct the light,

you allow me to see
the base of my love,
leaving me to stand with
wonder and light and
my love for the Sprite.

January 8, 2017

When Old Friends Meet

When old friends get together,
the efforts of travel fall away
at the moment of meeting.

It is a predictable scenario,
driven by duty to one another
and based on remembrance of who they were,
who they are, and who they will be.

Talk of family
evolves rapidly to talk of food:
what to eat,
how it was raised, grown,
and/or processed?

As always, the key to a life well-lived
is defined by food.
Humans fueled by the proper choice of calories,
display an effort to tune the body's
organic machinery to foster the growth of products
used in repairing worn-out parts.

Of course, the problems are: How do
you know it is working? And how
long do you have to wait for results?
Without an answer the concept is relegated
To *never mind*.

Old friends will newly discover
that reunion has always been about a way to be:
Relaxing, being aware in comfort while evaluating options,
using the expertise of others,
and being able to drop the shields
for ridicule and denigration.

For when love is present,
the luxury of life is apparent.
And the experiences
will be carried forward
for another day.

October 8, 2017

Our Great Honor and Privilege

Life's greatest honor and privilege is
to sleep with your lover
without care, knowing
they are there.

There is no place I would rather be.
For every night as my heart beats,
I slip beneath the sheets
and give thanks for my mate
and a place to lay my head.

Awestruck by her presence,
and stepping forward wrapped in love,
I am always available when requested,
a safety net with meaning.

Our compatibility is a wonder,
and it has always been there
as our spirits' joy,
since to us, it's no toy.

Together we are more than one or two.
There is me and you, and we. And we is
a creation arising from us two,
when we built its base with, "I do."

In our lives, privilege is granted
and honor is maintained, the fruits
of responsibility and great care. Thus avoiding
entitled arrogance and our undoing.

July 20, 2018

The Story of My Favorite Wife

My Grandfather used to say,
"When you tell a story,
it's best to begin with reality."

For a long time, I never expected
to have a wife, but I do.
We met in a chemistry class
at the University. Our mutual
attraction was instantaneous,
but binding took a while.

Now almost fifty years later,
I have one wife and she is my favorite.
There are other men who think,
"Having more than one wife
would be exotic and there would be
numerous choices for a favorite."

I think this is a false premise
because there were nearly
unlimited choices for marriage
to begin with, and adding more
does not offer more chance for happiness.

Be careful what you wish for.
Disparity in ages goes with choices, and
considering differences in energy levels,
by the time you could afford more than
one wife, you may only have one item
of interest between you.
And the desire may be one-sided.
What fun would that be?

I look at all my wife provides:
Her number-one talent is loving me.
Which includes my oddball
sense of humor and jokes.

GREG P. BUSACKER

She is consistently amazed
at my abilities to fix things broken or
things suffering from reduced performance.

To that end, she supports an accumulation
of incomprehensible tools. (As an aside,
it is always a good thing to know something
about how things work. Women appreciate it, too.
They are then able to tell their girlfriends
how lucky they are to have a man around
who knows so much.)

"I am exceedingly lucky
to share my life
with my favorite wife
and to be madly in love with her too.
I have never needed or wanted
more than one wife.
I chose a long time ago.
She was a beauty then
and she is a beauty now. I look at her
and I say, WOW!"

September 17, 2017

A Texas Woman

Last evening,
we watched a movie called *The Rookie*.
In the movie, when confronted
with adversity in supporting her husband,
his wife said, "I am a Texas woman
and I don't need a man
to keep things running."

Now we heard Carole K
make that call.
She wasn't in the movie
but we heard her
all the same, and
we are proud to know
this Texas woman.

We know where she stands:
all-in for family,
grandkids, and dogs;
plus she always
has time to love her friends.
People say, "Don't mess with Texas."
We say that means Carole K.
Now get out of her way!

Greg & Carol Busacker
November 17, 2016

MUSINGS

Full Circle

It seemed odd and perhaps it was.
For Father was born within sight
of the cemetery where he would lie.
As a boy, he had played there among
the tombstones.

This time he arrived in a box
carried by his son, daughter-in-law,
and an old friend. The day was overcast,
cold and nearly foggy. No one was
nearby and no one passed on the road.

They also carried a spade, a post-hole digger,
and a piece of plastic sheeting.
They walked to the grave site where his wife
lay waiting. Carefully removing a chunk of sod,
they used the post-hole digger to deepen the hole.
Then his ashes were poured in, and the dirt and grass were
replaced with hardly a trace of disturbance.

Heads bowed, they remembered the man and his wife
and walked away. Their work was scarcely noticeable,
and the plot was complete, as were they.

January 29, 2019

Waiting in the Doctor's Office

I am waiting in the doctor's office.
What to do? I could nap but
I would likely drool on my shirt.
No badge of honor there. Especially
when you are hoping to present yourself
as happy and well.

Examining the walls, I read of
opportunities for various medical
procedures for optimal health,
peace of mind, and vaccinations.

The examination table calls to me.
But I know I would leave a depression
in the paper covering, which would be
interpreted as an expression of weakness.

Why am I here? I could make the
same statement on my overall health
using the telephone, or even by mail
using a Forever stamp:

> "Dear Doctor X:
>
> I hope this note finds you
> enjoying the same level
> of robust health that I am.
>
> Forever yours,
>
> Patient Y
>
> P.S. I will follow up in six months."

July 12, 2019

A Glimpse of the Mortal Clock

He stumbled and fell;
it did not go well.
His body was
bruised and broken;
his spirit a bent token.

As he fell, he rolled but
the pipe stopped him cold.
He took it in his back
but he felt like it was a rack.
As he struggled, he managed to
stagger and stand,
while he evaluated his new pains. And
then—he heard the tick-tock
of the mortal clock.

He remembered a vision years ago,
seeing the clock through a crack in the door.
Now it seemed there was more.
The clock was bigger,
the tick-tock rapped louder with vigor,
but there were no booming chimes
to mark the end of his rhymes.

September 11, 2018

Gravity's Call: A Second Fall

Momentum
had delivered
a crumpled
body
into a pile
by the car,
suggesting
an arrested
somersault.
Head
twisted down,
bald pate
nestled
in gravel rocks,
left arm
under chest
with acute pain
radiating
from wrist,
knees supporting hips,
he was basically
unable to move.

How
did this happen?
Standing
one moment,
then lurching
two steps forward
only
to become
horizontal.
Bouncing
his forehead
off the
concrete patio,
while
jamming
his hand
on a car tire.

It
was surreal,
the magic
of motion
gone;
laid low,
he was
face to face
with gravity
and gravel.

Then it
was off to
Urgent Care,
a clean break
at the wrist.
No setting,
no surgery,
just
a cast
to allow
the bone
to heal.

The damages
were temporary
issues. But
he knew
gravity always
speaks, and the
message is clear.
Your balance
is key
in avoiding
gravity's embrace.

November 7, 2018

GREG P. BUSACKER

A Broken Wrist

I think I broke my wrist.
Doc says, "Make a fist."
"Not today."
"Sign the OK?"
"Nope."
"Wiggle your fingers?"

Diminished capacity,
it seems I have broken my wrist.
It looks misshapen and hurts like hell.

The x-ray lady comes by.
Big woman, big machine,
She ramps up her machine and my pain,
but she shoots good pictures.

The Ortho Doc comes by.
Shows me the pictures.

Says, "We can set this for now, but
surgery is recommended for a lasting fix."

"I'll tell you a secret.
I don't like the thought of surgery.
I can hardly stand needles,
let alone knives."

Doc says, "I'll give you a nerve block
and we will reset your wrist."

Working by the sink, he pulls out a gigantic needle,

"Not that!" I say.

"Oh, that's just for mixing, I have a smaller one."

It might be smaller but it is three inches long and
the syringe is as big as a roll of quarters.

"As I inject the block into the area of the break,
this will only hurt a little.
You will feel a sharp pain followed by pressure."

"You have to be kidding me."
He lied of course;
it hurt like hell and I thought he would never quit.
So I asked him, "What do you do when the patient begs
you to stop?"

"Nothing. Mostly I don't listen.
I make the patient as comfortable as possible
And then I do what needs to be done."

When injected with an anti-anxiety drug,
I screamed, "I don't have anxiety!
Did I tell you I don't like needles?"

Finally, they brought in a contraption
with hanging tubes, reminding me
of Chinese finger traps.
I soon find my hand, wrist, and arm,
hanging from the tubes with my wrist
slowly moving back into shape.

The splint looks benign,
plaster on two sides,
lots of padding, just for four days until surgery.
It's okay until he takes my arm and wrist for final position,
and bends my wrist over his knee like firewood.
Unpleasant is a kind word.

As for future surgery, I can hardly wait.
But now I can make a fist,
wiggle and spread my fingers,
and not last or least,
sign okay.

By the way, if you find yourself falling,
have the wit to keep your hands out of the way.

July 19, 2015

A Tribute to Mary Berry

For the University of Nebraska Rifle Team

Mary Berry was one
of the Goddesses of Iowa,
blonde hair, well built,
super smart, with a razor-sharp wit.

She was the second oldest of nine,
always taking responsibility
for what was wanted and needed.
She was unflappable in times of crisis.

She had a deep drive
to serve her people. It was an
audacious undertaking, because
her people numbered in the
thousands. Many of them were
students in her classes.

Believing in the profession of education,
she stood out, for she took pride
in her students and their accomplishments.
She loved teaching teenagers. She demanded
performance which they gave her.
She was their teacher; but there was also reciprocity,
as they taught her too.
Laughter was a major part of her classes,
because she used her classes and subject matter
to teach students how to live, tempering
their dreams and their pains with wisdom.

When school shootings became an issue,
she became licensed for concealed carry,
and packed a pistol in her purse.
She was determined to not be put off
by violence and she was determined
to protect herself and her students.

Mary worked hard at whatever
she was doing. At the University of
Nebraska, she supported herself
as a manager of The Dog and Suds,
as a nanny, and as a waitress, and
manager of an interstate truck stop
between Lincoln and Omaha.
She made life-long friends from
those arrangements.

In the mid-nineteen sixties, she
met Tom and they became a
couple. At times, she seemed to be fixated
on tying Tom down, and he
did things that drove her mad.
I suppose it was a form of avoidance,
but perseverance in matters of love
was a strong point with Mary;
they eventually married
and raised two fine young men.

After her passing, former members
of the University of Nebraska Rifle Team
sat for remembrance and awe. They
realized she was one of them.
She did not shoot for fun in competition,
but she was a rock supporting them in their
activities. For gatherings of many or few
she was always glad to see them, and
hear stories of their lives. In the end,
all their memories were folded into
remembrances, love, and recognition
of how fortunate they had been
to be part of Mary's life.

Attending Members:

| Tom Berry | Jim Brown | Greg Busacker |
| Richard Christensen | Howard McNiff | Marvin Cox |

October 27, 2018

Milestone

The day his father died,
he was ill, and in his bed,
when the nurse called and said,
"I am afraid your father
has passed away. When
I went to check on him,
I found him in his chair.
He was still warm,
but his spirit
was no longer there."

Totally surprised was he.
The news left him
wondering how to be.
There were people
to call and tell the news.

As he sat on the stairs,
he was swept with the blues
and racked with grief.
He was the last living
member of his family,
and with mother and sister
already gone he thought they already knew.
So he called his wife and they
made plans of what to do.

Who knew?

March 29, 2019

The Fourth Quarter: Memories of Mother

Inspired by Ted Kooser's Poem "Mother."
Kindest Regards; *Copper Canyon Press, 2018.*

Mother, it is May and the peonies are blooming.
Memorial Day is barreling down the dusty roads
we traveled, leading to isolated cemeteries in the
countryside's new green.

Every spring, you taught me to honor the memories of our families.
We would cut the red, white and pink blossoms
from the cheerful peony bushes, stuff them into buckets
and Mason jars wrapped in tinfoil,
then transport them to burial sites,
where we would lay them at the headstones of people,
some I knew briefly, some I knew well, and many I never
knew beyond your stories.
Then we would kneel in the newly mown grass
and pray for them.

In time, I rebelled and said, "I am to be cremated, and my
ashes scattered from the air over the Nebraska Sand Hills—
far from the dusty roads and glacial hills of eastern Nebraska."

Mother, I want you to know, I gave that up and I will now lie
in the family plot, with people I loved, and people I never met,
but loved for their contribution to my life.

Today my tears wet the grass. My time is coming,
it's the fourth quarter,
the game-ending points are yet to be scored, and thanks to you,
I am a winner.

March 27, 2017

The Illusion of Dignity

Awake in the night
he headed for the bathroom
using a recently acquired cane.
But still, he found himself
freezing at corners.

With the cane's support,
he hoped he would confer
a little dignity to his trip,
as he was more erect in his stride.

He stopped near a mirror,
not to trim his mustache,
rather to negotiate a turn.
His feet gave a semblance
of attentive evaluation.

But his feet were going nowhere.
The frontal areas of his thighs
felt newly leaden and they failed
to execute his demands.

With his stutter-stepping feet,
he slowly rotated. Then the way
was clear, and he shouted "Forward."

The left foot stepped over
the grouted tile line, as the
right foot and cane moved
simultaneously rearward.

Off again, he lacked
only a bowler hat
and an umbrella
to add status to his walk.

He was so pleased with
his progress, he nearly
forgot his destination in
the bathroom.

As the long-sought release
rushed forward, he thought,
Ah well, there is still the return
trip to dignify my nocturnal self.

November 1, 2017

Falls

The doctors told me, I had a neurodegenerative
disease and I would fall without warning.
I did not believe them.
Maybe you, but not me, Doc.
I have had a lifetime of athletic activity, and I
have done things you have not dreamed of.

Arrogance brought up short;
I fell without warning each time.
Five falls over eleven months, both wrists
broken, and one hip broken.
The last fall cost two surgeries, six days
in the hospital, and ten days rehabilitation—
with outpatient rehabilitation yet to come.

I have experienced a teaching moment, leaving me stymied.

June 15, 2019

Lost Opportunities

My Mother, Millicent: (April, 2003)
You were the first to go and you were
my first love. I want to acknowledge your
early family actions. As a young mother
you stepped up without complaint taking care
of me, Patricia, and Dad. You carved homes
from the five houses we lived in when we moved
to Nebraska. Early conditions were primitive and
at days' end, you were spent but always available.

My Sister, Patricia: (December 2004)
You went next and I never fully expressed to you
how proud I am of you and your accomplishments
in your profession, in choosing Jim as a life partner,
and how much I appreciate your love for me.

My Father, Harold: (April 2005)
You were third and your sudden death took me
by surprise. I admired your incredible drive and
inventiveness as an engineer. I was thrilled with
your love for Mom, Patricia, and me. You also
demonstrated your love for your greater family,
which has inspired me to find family and enjoy those
relationships wherever I go. And finally, thank you
for your unabashed support for me
when I doubted my own gifts.

Carol's Mother, Alleen: (June 2005)
You were next. I wanted to tell you
how grateful I am to have had Carol
partially trained when we were married.
She is a loving head-strong woman.
I could not have asked for more.
You took me into your family as a full-fledged
member right from the start, and I knew it was so.
Also, Carol is responsible for me being me.

Carol's Father, Clarence: (August 2005)
I never acknowledged you for being the epitome
of a loving family man, able to look around
disappointment and disapproval to keep your love
of family alive. Thank you for the wild and rebellious
woman I had the privilege to marry. You shaped her
as best you could. And you allowed me
to discover how great she is.
Thank you for your unstinting love and support!

July 15, 2019

The Daily Dilemma

The day begins—I am awake, sluggish,
posture stooped, and moving slowly
using a cane. The first cocktail taken,
I am waiting for the drugs to have
a positive effect, to loosen my gait
and allow my thoughts to be elsewhere.
Thus setting a course of action
for using the remaining body to its fullest extent.

Damage to the body can take awhile,
or it can happen in the blink of an eye.
The end result is part mannequin,
and part diminished capacity.
Hundreds of millions have gone before me.
I know they endured, with
parts of their bodies missing,
or just not working well, or
not functioning at all. So I can too.

If I compare myself to my toys,
without external intervention,
they are motionless. I don't
need a push, just a potion
of chemicals so my brain can
talk to my limbs.

Then I am able to move almost
"normally." But I have a
duty to track the next chemical dose
and take it on time or
suffer diminished performance.
I have a vibrating watch on my wrist
alerting me to the time to take pills,
and that helps. All in all, I think

I get around fairly well.
But people rush to open doors for me.
I am grateful, but always surprised.
I thought I was a regular guy.

By midday the cane is
set aside and my thoughts
and actions focus on some task.
My penmanship is more legible.
I now have eight to twelve hours,
excluding meals to accomplish
something.

What will it be?

May 25, 2018

Tai Chi Chuan

On hearing the news,
he got up and started Tai Chi.

The movement quiet and controlled,
the motions distinguishing nothing,
but moving to something
defined in the different postures.

He generated a sense
of flowing wind interrupted
by standing meditations.

When the news became old he stopped.
Refreshed,
he had become one with reality.

Prepared for
Mary Cruise

May 13, 2017

Rachael Wittenberger, P.T.

(Trained in Method Osteopathic Manipulation)

Rachael,
your skills expose
who you are
in your stand
for all.

Believing
efficiency of movement
is possible at any level,
the expression
of mind, body, and spirit
is evidence of one's
current state.

We move freely under your care,
not locked and stooped, but
standing tall and loose.

Resignation is in the past,
leaving us as carefree
and moving like a child.

December, 2017

The Magic Carpet

A Nod to Geetha Davis, MD Ophthalmology, University of Missouri

Years ago,
an operation on my eyes
was unthinkable.

Now I ride
the magic carpet of trust
powered by my surgeon.
While any surgery has risks,
there is ease with my vision
of a better future.

But to get there, it is
off to the operating room,
where they roll you out, and
the next thing you remember
is the nurses congratulating you
on a job well done.

Hmmm?

What do they give you
that has you remain conscious
yet erases your mind?

That not withstanding,
I can see,
high and low,
near and far,
yes, it is going to be a great ride.

Thank you, Doctor Davis!

March 3, 2016

Memorial Day 2017

On this day we gather together to honor the dead.
Those who have gone before us,
those who sacrificed for us,
and even those who had little concept of community.
All contributed to where we stand today.

For the veterans we honor, it is simple;
all gave some, some gave all.
For those who now serve, we pray they return safely,
so we can honor and thank them.

For the countless relatives who shaped our lives,
we thank them for the life they gave us.
For we now have the choice of how we live
our remaining time. For our friends
and neighbors both living and dead,
thank you for your contributions to our lives.

No matter your age, the day is coming
when your contributions will be honored and acknowledged.
We offer you a thank you in advance.
For you standing here now, know your life matters
to family, friends and neighbors, and countless others.

For this is a day we walk forward with gratitude,
building for today and tomorrow.

Go with God.

May 25, 2017

The Appointment

Today he was early for his appointment.
Not surprising, he was almost never late.
He waited wondering about the timing
of his visit and the scheduled therapy.

Other patients in the waiting area
told their stories with a little prodding
and he listened, providing a clearing
for what they had to say.

When they were done, he would read them
one of his own poems, trying to match their
experiences and resonance to that of the poetry.
If he were able to make the match,
the glue holding their tale together fell away.

This gave them a new beginning
with another interpretation of life.
Pain and angst were reduced or absent,
and they were able to experience a forgotten
quality of living.

January 6, 2020

Wishing You Well

A book of writing
covering myriad thoughts
and vivid images.

May this little book
bring you healing grace and love.
So you may know peace.

Indeed, be well soon.
For your smile banishes night
as you are light.

July 1, 2019

The Mythos of Twenty–Twenty: A Report

It was January first in the mythic date of twenty-twenty.

In the 1950s when I dreamed of space travel,
magazines predicted off-world excursions would be
available two decades into the new millennium.

I wondered what I would be doing then?

The results of my look into the future were cloudy.

I have lived a long time. The days have not been trivial.
I have grown and evolved. But I am not traveling off-world.

Space travel is confined
to my surroundings and my imagination.

The myth has not changed.

January 1, 2020

GREG P. BUSACKER

About the Author

Greg P. Busacker was born in Missouri and raised in Nebraska. He holds a BS in Zoology from the University of Nebraska at Lincoln, an MA in Fisheries Biology from the University of Missouri at Columbia, a PhD in Biological Sciences from Wayne State University in Detroit, and did postdoctoral work at the University of Minnesota.

Greg worked as a Natural Resource Specialist for the Minnesota Department of Transportation. He served in the 101st Airborne Division of the US Army as a Helicopter Mechanic and Paratrooper.

He and his wife, Carol live on a small tree farm in Central Missouri. They have one daughter and son-in-law living in Southern California.

www.ingramcontent.com/pod-product-compliance
Lightning Source LLC
Chambersburg PA
CBHW062108080426
42734CB00012B/2797